The Knitter's Gift

An inspirational bag of words, wisdom, and craft

Edited by

Bernadette Murphy ·

Adams Media

Avon, Massachusetts

For John, Jarrod, Neil, and Hope,
who give the fibers of my life shape and meaning.

Published by
Adams Media, an F+W Publications Company
57 Littlefield Street, Avon, MA 02322. U.S.A.
www.adamsmedia.com

ISBN: 1-59337-100-4

Printed in Canada.

J I H G F E D C B A

Library of Congress Cataloging-in-Publication Data
The knitter's gift / edited by Bernadette Murphy.
p.   cm.
ISBN 1-59337-100-4
1. Knitting. 2. Knitters (Persons) I. Murphy, Bernadette.
TT820.K69455 2004
813'.0108357—dc22
2004009166

Interior illustrations by Eric Andrews.

This book is available at quantity discounts for bulk purchases.
For information, call 1-800-872-5627.

Contents

Acknowledgments

A HUGE THANK-YOU TO ALL the writers and knitters who shared their stories with me and made this collection possible. I am honored and humbled to have served as the midwife birthing your stories, poems, and experiences into the world. Thank you for your trust in me.

Thanks as well to all the usual suspects: the Tuesday night Tao ladies—Michelle, Cathy, Kate, Tracy, and Cindy—who remind me of what's important in life; my writing circle—Marjorie, Kitty, Michelle, Tara, and David—who keep me sane and returning to the keyboard; the editors of the *Los Angeles Times Book Review*, whose regular assignments keep me reading and solvent; the administrators of the UCLA Extension Writers Program, who continue to ask me back to teach, thereby allowing me to enrich my life by giving what I have received; to my intrepid agent, Bonnie Nadell, who talks me down when I need it; to my editor, Kate Epstein, who keeps me on track; and to all the knitters and writers who have come before me. My needles are raised in salute to you.

Introduction

Two years ago, I released a book about my own spiritual and creative experience as a knitter—*Zen and the Art of Knitting*—that allowed me to look into aspects of knitting I'd always been curious about and to express my own perspective on this graceful and venerable craft. When that book came out, I was amazed by the number of knitters who'd identified with my experience and then wanted to share their own. Knitters approached me in bookstores, over the Internet, at seminars, wanting to share with me the most precious gift they had: the tales of their own adventures, tribulations, coincidences, and anecdotes of knitting.

This collection represents some of those stories, as well as insights from other knitters and writers generous enough to offer what they, too, have to share.

It is my fervent hope that, whether or not you're a knitter, you will find some aspect of your own story reflected here. Pull up a chair, drape an afghan over your legs, and enter this world. It is a realm in which a pair of needles and a single strand of yarn ties the generations together, a place where the wounds of the human condition are salved, a source of warmth on days when our souls shiver, and a moment to remind ourselves of the importance of the small things in life.

One: Knit with the Past

"Most people have an obsession: mine is knitting."
—ELIZABETH ZIMMERMAN, *Knitting Without Tears*

Hand-knit sweaters, booties, socks, shawls, afghans—
these items, often delicate and painstakingly created, are not simply functional objects that serve a particular
purpose. The things we hand-knit are greater than the sum of
their parts; in many ways, they are so much more.

First, there's the wool from which hand-knit items are made,
bringing with them an ingrained story of sheep life, before this
current incarnation as cloth. Then there's the person who
carded and spun the wool, whose own relationship to the
sheep we may know well, or just speculate about. Maybe
the yarn was mass-produced; still, someone selected the
dye colors, someone tested the machines, and someone
threw the switch to set the spinning into motion. Then
there's the person who made the item,
knitter, who trails behind her the thread

of a unique history. Her own experience of learning to knit—the relationship between knitting teacher and pupil—is a connection inherent in each stitch and every cast-off. Finally, there's the dance of give-and-take between the knitter and the intended wearer of the item: One provides warmth and love in the form of the knitted garment, while the other plays just as important a role by a willingness to receive the gift. Each of us must be both, givers and receivers, for the cycle to continue.

Hand-knit speaks to relationship. It's no coincidence that a family may be characterized as "close-knit." From the sheep to the spinner, from the knitting-shop owner to the knitter, from the creator to the intended wearer, knitting is about strengthening ties, about acknowledging connectedness. Knitting is about family, yes, but also about embracing those not related by blood or law, but by love and choice, celebrating the people who have become friends-that-are-like-family, or "framily."

Knitting makes manifest the love of a mother passed on to her child, or the concern of an older relative for her young cousin. It enables a daughter to show her larger-than-life father the devotion she feels but cannot name, except in knitted stitches. John McCann's "The Big Sweater" recounts how, in the Irish tradition, knitted designs were embedded in sweaters, like a coat of arms, to identify the family from which the pattern originated. This knitting also had the darker purpose of allowing easy identification of a fisherman drowned at sea.

All knitting, ultimately, speaks to that abiding truth: Mortality is a fact of life, and while we're here and moving and able, we'll knit all the love and joy, all the awe and wonder we feel into each and every sweater, hat, mitten, and sock we make. We are all linked by the stories we tell, by the myths we share, by the way we knit ourselves together.

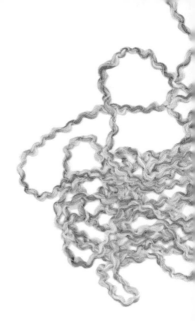

my father's scarf

My father sold tungsten carbide cutting tools—"strong enough to cut a diamond," he would proudly report. As a sales engineer, he'd carry his products in and out of factories filled with machines larger than dinosaurs. Winters in Springfield, Ohio, often blew biting winds that drifted snow up the sides of buildings. I was a Girl Scout in fifth grade at Snowhill Elementary School, trying to earn more badges on my sash. I loved to finger the glossy embroidery inside each circle and imagine my sash ablaze with patches.

I decided that if I learned how to knit, I could knit my father a scarf to accompany him on his sales routes, especially those that took him away for nights at a time. Charcoal gray seemed serious enough to wear to work and would match his black tweed coat, bridging the gap between his collar and the felt-brimmed hat sporting a fan-shaped pheasant feather. After painstakingly knitting several rows, I saw that the scarf would be too wide. I feared if I started over I would lose heart and not begin again, so I lowered my head and knit into this scratchy gray expanse, trying to earn a new identity as "resourceful," like my grandmothers.

My father was handsome in a Bing Crosby kind of way, able to dance and sing with grace. He would sing "I am I, Don Quixote, the Lord of La Mancha," one moment and "Moon River" the next. Often, when he was worn out from work and hours of driving, we four children would prove overwhelming to him. His temper would flare and his irascibility would erupt—"I'll give you something to cry about!" Yet he was the sentimental one, the one who could receive a present with sincere appreciation. "He's charming," my mom would concede begrudgingly, "but the man you enjoy at a party is usually the man you don't want to take home with you and certainly don't want to live with every day." The house would sometimes shake with their anger. I nurtured the hope of making a present that could erase the wrongs and fill in the gaps. As their marriage unraveled, I imagined knitting the crinkled yarn into the scarf.

My father watched with close attention as the scarf grew row by painstaking row. He asked questions with interest and encouragement as it grew loop by loop, sometimes with a hole or knot and cut yarn—mounting evidence that I was not now and never would be handy. I would mutter Madame Defarge–like into my web of scarf that this was the first and last thing I would ever make. Yet in spite of these protests, the stitches diligently—though unevenly—kept accruing. Trying to make conversation, my father would tilt his head and finger the rows of knitting, asking, "How long do you think this will take you? You're working awfully hard," as if I were running up a hill. In the summer he asked, "Will it be ready for the falling leaves?" At Christmas, past the goal, he asked, "How about Valentine's Day?"

When I finished knitting the scarf, my father treated it as the wonder that it was, a handmade gift filled with loops intended for him. How clearly that first putting on of the scarf remains in my mind's eye! Securing one end of the scarf, he deliberately wound it with a staged presence, sustaining eye contact with me as he slowly lifted it. He examined each row of knitting, fingering the bumps and ridges, and shook his head admiringly, as if in my act of knitting I had created a world marvelous and new. He wound that too-wide gray scarf several circles around his neck, working some space with his finger between the high mound of scratchy wool and his stifled neck. Dad wore this hairshirt of his fathering more patiently than he endured my persistent questions and my intense stares of resistance to his barked commands. This wearing of the homemade scarf he could do with grace and élan, and although I flinched to see him buried beneath the broad coils of love, I felt in his cheerful endurance of this ungainly scarf a certain acceptance of me.

The scarf is still in my father's possession, enduring long after his marriage to my mother. He even wore it with his glamorous second wife, who once made a condescending remark about it. We knew silently that her beauty could not cover her lack of emotional warmth and delicacy. And now his third and enduring wife—his true love match—appreciates the scarf and the man who wears it.

My fifth-grade son, Isaac, asked me recently if a friend of ours could teach us how to knit. Isaac has red hair and freckles, and he likes to give presents. When my voice rises in frustration from everyone making demands at once, his eyes drop down and his lips tremble. He has also, like me, taken on the peace-making role. As our friend shows us how to knit, the muscles in my fingers, like someone playing the violin or piano, remember more quickly than the mind, and soon the silver knitting needle slides under the loop and behind the left needle, as the click and tap guide me. The rhythm of sounds drops me back in time even as I burrow into this present moment. I slide the loop up the pole, remembering these sounds of earlier years, imagining the knitting binding the generations together, odd and even, and in spite of missed stitches and often knotted yarn, adding on to the band of love.

Leah Buturain Schneider

"Life is a thread that is never broken, never lost. Do you know why? Because each man makes a knot in the thread during his lifetime: it is the work he has done and that's what gives life to life in the long stretch of time: the usefulness of man on this earth."

—JACQUES ROUMAIN

six and counting

In 1964, when I was nine, I had a favorite sweater. The thing I liked most about it was that it was blue. Not baby blue, but a grown-up blue. Not navy blue, not royal blue—it was sky blue, but not the washed-out sky blue of a spring morning or even the light-and-bright sky blue of a July afternoon. It was the exact blue of an autumn day almost verging on winter, deep without being dark, that perfect color of blue that is not cobalt and not periwinkle, but contains elements of both. It was a substantial sweater, made of a twisted, heavy-gauge yarn, with a large, square collar like that on a child's sailor suit. The collar was fringed around the edges, and there were big blue buttons down the front. There was something about this sweater that made me feel special every time I put it on. It was stylish but practical, and flattering to my blonde hair. I wore the sweater for two years on every possible occasion, beginning with the sleeves rolled up into cuffs and letting go of it only when the ends of its sleeves crept above my wrist bones and it no longer closed down the front. At that point I reluctantly allowed my mother to wash and block it one last time before placing it in tissue paper in a footlocker in the attic, to wait. I was not the last person to wear the sweater, nor was I the first.

ꙮꙮ

In the summer of 1958, my cousin Carol Sue Walker was nineteen years old. She had just completed her first year at Boston University, and she was living at home in Salisbury, Massachusetts, with her mother and her younger brother and sister while commuting to college. It was a tough first year. In between classes and after 3 p.m., she worked as a secretary's helper in the registrar's office for sixty-five cents an hour. On Fridays she left early and spent Friday night, Saturday, and Sunday morning working as a waitress at Ye Cocke & Kettle. In this way she paid for her commuting expenses, books, clothes, and whatever college fees were not covered by her three scholarships.

Carol Sue's father was no longer in the picture, and her mother, Edith, was supporting her family by doing housecleaning. During the summer, Carol Sue had planned to waitress full-time, putting aside funds for the coming year, but one of her sorority sisters, Richardine Minnig, invited Carol Sue to spend the three-month break at her home in upstate New York. "Dean" lived in the Catskills, in a small town called Liberty, with her parents, two sisters, and two brothers. Dean had worked during previous summers at Smitty's, a soda shop just down the road from Grossinger's, a popular kosher golf and ski resort. She promised Carol Sue that they could both work at Smitty's and would earn a lot in tips. Carol Sue, who needed a break from the tense atmosphere created by her parents' divorce, agreed.

The hours at Smitty's were irregular. Sometimes the girls would pull the morning shift and have their afternoon and evening free, while other days they'd start work at 2:00 p.m. and work until midnight. The two didn't always get called for the same shift, leaving Carol Sue, a stranger in town, with some hours to fill. She decided to fill them by knitting a sweater for her sister, Anne, who was a petite eleven years old that summer.

Carol Sue had learned to knit at the age of nine. In her small town there were no Girl Scout troops, so the little girls joined the 4H Club as "Clover Buds." Instead of raising calves and lambs, the typical pursuit of 4H-er boys, they learned the household skills so highly emphasized in those postwar years. Local mothers took a turn at teaching their particular talents, and Carol Sue and the other girls learned to knit, crochet, sew, and cook. Every summer the Clover Buds would take the nonperishable products of their industry to the Topsfield County Fair, where the crafts were displayed alongside the fat pigs and woolly sheep the boys had brought. During and after her 4H career, Carol Sue had knitted scarves, hats, gloves, and vests, but this was to be her first sweater.

The sweater was Style No. 5955 from Book 68 of the Bernat Handicrafter (Bulky Knits for Girls and Boys), and the yarn was called Bernat Cuddlespun. She picked the heavy yarn and the pattern with the ample collar hoping that it would keep her sister warmer than the average sweater would. Winters were cold in Salisbury, and the meager family budget didn't always stretch far enough for much coal, after $16 per week had been spent on rent. The sweater took Carol Sue about a month to knit, and she presented it to Anne in September after she returned home from the Catskills. Anne, whose favorite color was blue, was delighted with it. She wore it the first day of sixth grade and for a couple of years thereafter.

In 1961, after graduating from a two-year program at Boston University, Carol Sue moved to northern California and enrolled at the

University of California. She lived in Berkeley for three years. Her only relative on the West Coast was her mother's youngest sister, Bernice, who was fourteen years older than Carol Sue and who lived down south in Riverside with her husband, Joe, and their daughter—me. During those three years, Carol Sue often caught a commuter flight down to Riverside for a weekend visit with us. She always brought some little gift for me—bubble bath, cologne, a book, a doll—and

Anne models her gift from Carol Sue.

every once in a while brought along a boyfriend as well, for a steak dinner on the patio and Aunt Bernie and Uncle Joe's stamp of approval. She was still knitting, but she had discovered a disturbing trend: Every time she knitted a sweater for a boyfriend, they broke up.

In 1964, Carol Sue found herself at a crossroads: She had been dating a man who had moved to Los Angeles to work at Rocketdyne in the San Fernando Valley, and she was finding a long-distance relationship difficult to maintain. All her friends from Cal Berkeley had graduated and left, and she decided she must either return to Massachusetts—where she would have to find a job, a roommate, and a place to live—or go to Los Angeles to room with a friend there, and be near boyfriend Mike and her California family. She chose Los Angeles. That year, she visited her mother in Massachusetts, and she brought back Anne's outgrown blue sweater for me to wear, cautioning my mother not to give it away when I outgrew it in turn. She also knitted Mike a sweater, and the relationship ended.

Early in 1965, friends of Carol Sue's introduced her to Walter Kaufmann, a young widower with a two-year-old daughter named Karen. She refused to knit him a sweater, and they married in August of that year. Ten months later, their daughter Heidi was born, followed twenty-seven months after that by another daughter, Kirsten. In 1972, during one of the family's visits to Riverside, my mother mentioned to Carol Sue that she still had Anne's (and my) blue sweater stored away in the attic, and she thought it would now fit Karen. Out it came, and down it went: two years with Karen, two years with Heidi, two years with Kirsten. It had become a family rite of passage, the blue sweater one wore from ages nine to eleven and passed to the next candidate.

Back in Massachusetts, Anne had married John Manson and given birth to a daughter, Heather, in 1972, and a son, Corey, in 1975. In 1981, the blue sweater flew back across the country to keep nine-year-old Heather warm through two years of East Coast winters.

The author, Melissa, in 1964, wearing the handed-down sweater.

ⵊⵉⵉⵉⵉ

Since the early 1980s, our family has had a shortage of nine-year-old, sweater-wearing girls. Heather is now thirty-one, and the sweater is lying in wait for her daughter, Emily, eighteen months old, to grow into the legacy that unspooled from the knitting needles of her great-aunt in 1958 to provide warmth for six little girls over five decades.

Carol Sue is still knitting, and she attributes her thirty-eight-year marriage to the fact that not once has she knitted anything for Walter—not a scarf, not a hat, not a sock, and certainly not a sweater.

Melissa Garrison Elliott

Child's Chunky Sweater
by Bernat

(*reprinted by permission of Bernat Yarns*)

For child's size 8. Changes for child's sizes 10 and 12 are in parentheses.

MATERIALS:

- Bernat Softee Chunky (2-oz. skeins) 7 (8-8)
- 1 pair each straight knitting needles Nos. 4 and 9
  (or any size needles that will give the stitch gauge given below)
- 1 steel crochet hook No. 00
- 7 buttons
- 1½ yds. 1½-inch grosgrain ribbon

The pattern for the sweater pictured below was published in this 1958 Bernat pattern book.

GAUGE: 4 sts = 1 inch, 6 rows = 1 inch

PATTERN STITCH: Multiple of 5 sts plus 4
Row 1: K4 *P1, K4, repeat from * across row.
Row 2: Purl
Repeat these 2 rows for pattern stitch.

BACK: Using No. 4 needles, cast on 38 (44–48) sts. K1, P1 in ribbing for 2 inches, inc 1(0–1) st at end of last row—39 (44–49) sts.
Change to No. 9 needles and work in pattern st, inc 1 st each end
of needle every ½ inch 8 (7–7) times, forming new patterns as sts
are increased. Work even on 55 (58–63) sts until piece measures 10
(10½–11) inches. SHAPE ARMHOLES: At the beg of each of the next
2 rows bind off 3 (3–4) sts. Dec 1 st at each end of the needle every
other row 3 times. Work even on 43 (46–49) sts until armholes measure 5½ (6½–6½) inches. SHAPE SHOULDERS: At the beg of each of
the next 2 rows bind off 7 sts. At the beg of each of the next 2 rows
bind off 6 (7–8) sts. Bind off remaining 17 (18–19) sts.

LEFT FRONT: Using No. 4 needles, cast on 24 (26–29) sts. Row 1: K1,
P1 in ribbing for 19 (19–24) sts, K5 (7–5) for front band. Row 2: K5
(7–5), work in ribbing on last 19 (19–24) sts. Repeat these 2 rows for 2
inches, ending with Row 2. Change to No. 9 needles. Work in pattern
st on first 19 (19–24) sts, sl last 5 (7–5) sts onto a holder to be worked

later for front band. Continue in pattern st, inc 1 st at arm edge every ½ inch 8 (7–7) times, forming new patterns as sts are increased. Work even on 27 (26–31) sts until piece measures 10 (10½–11) inches. **SHAPE ARMHOLE:** At arm edge bind off 3 (3–4) sts. Dec 1 st at same edge every other row 3 times. Work even on 21 (20–24) sts until armhole measures 4½ (4½–5½) inches. **SHAPE NECK:** At front edge bind off 5 (3–6) sts. Dec 1 st at neck edge every other row 3 times. Work even on 13 (14–15) sts until armhole measures 5½ (6½–6½) inches. **SHAPE SHOULDER:** At arm edge bind off 7 sts once and 6 (7–8) sts once. **LEFT FRONT BAND:** Sl 5 (7–5) sts of front band onto No. 4 needle. Join yarn at inner edge and continue in garter st until piece is same length as front to start of neck shaping. Bind off.

RIGHT FRONT AND RIGHT FRONT BAND: Work to correspond to left front and left front band, reversing all shaping and forming first buttonhole when piece measures ½ inch. **BUTTONHOLE:** Starting at right front edge, K1(3–1), bind off next 2 sts, work to end of row. On next row cast on 2 sts over those bound off on previous row. Make 6 more buttonholes, evenly spaced—the last one to be made ½ inch below start of neck shaping.

SLEEVES: Using No. 4 needles, cast on 28 (30–32) sts. K1, P1 in ribbing for 3 inches. P1 row, inc at even intervals to 34 sts. Change to No. 9 needles and work in pattern st, inc 1 st each end of needle every 1½ inches 4 (6–7) times, forming new pattern as sts are increased. Work even on 42 (46–48) sts until piece measures 12½ (13½–15) inches. **SHAPE CAP:** At the beg of each of the next 2 rows bind off

3 (3–4) sts. Dec I st each end of needle every other row 8 (11–11) times and every 4th row I (0–1) time. At the beg of each of the next 6 rows bind off 2 sts. Bind off remaining sts.

COLLAR: Using No. 9 needles, cast on 49 (54–59) sts. Work even in pattern st for 3 inches. SHAPE NECK: Work 16 (18–20) sts, join another ball of yarn and bind off center 17 (18–19) sts, work last 16 (18–20) sts. Working on both sides at once, at each neck edge bind off 4 sts 3 times. At each neck edge bind off remaining 4 (6–8) sts of each side.

FINISHING: Sew underarm and sleeve seams. Set in sleeves. Sew front bands in place. Sew collar to within 3 sts of each front edge. With right side facing you, work I row single crochet on each front edge. Work 2 rows single crochet around outer edges of collar, inc in corners. FRINGE: Cut strands of yarn 5 inches long. Knot I strand in each of the single crochet stitches of collar. Steam. Face fronts with ribbon. Finish buttonholes. Sew on buttons. ●

the big sweater

Cleaning out a closet one day, I found a massive sweater. This turtleneck was so heavy you could wear it as part of a set of full-body armor. I hadn't seen that knit sweater in almost twenty years— and for good reason. Big wool garments are about as practical in Southern California as iron surfboards. Still, it brought back memories of my mother and our unique family history, stretching back over a century.

My mother was a knitter from a long line of Irish knitters, learning the skill from her mother, Grandma Fielding. Grandma Fielding, in turn, learned from her mother, who was said to have been deported to Australia for knitting a lewd bonnet.

Youngest of six, my Mom was born in 1919 on a farm in County Kilkenny. The 1920s and '30s were tough times for the Fieldings and Ireland. Rebellion against Great Britain spun off a civil war that ended just in time for an economic downturn. Years of trouble spawned a wave of depressing ballads, and soon the entire Emerald Isle was singing about how awful things were. I still have the LPs.

Mom's three brothers were committed to working the farm and arguing. Her two older sisters emigrated to America. A Chicago relative took them in, making the girls swear an oath to vote Democratic as often as possible. Mom's traditional options were to follow her sisters to America, stay home and be an unpaid drudge, or get married. Instead, she chose World War II.

Mom was under more sustained aerial bombardment than most guys at the local VFW bar ever were. She'd gone to London in 1939 to train as a nurse. Arriving in time for war, she put her new medical skills to use treating casualties during the Battle of Britain. By 1944, Mom was a British Army nursing officer working under the threat of Nazi V-2 rockets. These faster-than-sound missiles would obliterate a city block before you even heard their whooshing approach. In later years, Mom would freeze at any sudden crashing sound, such as her fumble-fingered children breaking the dishes. It took me a long time to realize that I had the only mother on the block suffering from Post-Traumatic Stress Disorder.

Mom arrived in Chicago after the war. She reunited with her sisters, nursed at St. Francis Hospital, and, in 1950, married a stubborn Irishman named Ted McCann. Ted (or "Dad" as I liked to call him) worked for the post office and moonlighted at various times as a security guard, deliveryman, and plumber. In later years, he taught me the value of hard work—or would have if I hadn't been hiding somewhere, reading comic books.

During the Kennedy Administration, the family—Mom, Dad, brother Tim, sister Mary Pat, and I—moved from Chicago to a house in suburban Skokie. Dad took up supervisory duties at the post office, which back then was still an unarmed organization. Mom clocked in as an industrial nurse at a huge company that made Teletype business machines. It was feast or famine nursing: You were either reading the newspaper or else some guy had just got his arm crinkled in heavy machinery. Mom didn't fancy any more traumas than necessary, so she worked the quieter swing shifts and overnights. I think this was the first time in years Mom had time to knit, because she needled up a storm. Before long we were in The Golden Age of Hats.

Over the next few years, everyone got a Mom-knit hat. I was a paperboy then. In the winter, temperatures of fifteen below were common and my breath plumed as if I were a young, steam-powered lad. My first knit hat was blue wool and heavy. If I weren't careful, my head would drop into elliptical loops like the moon. But it was pretty darn warm and the looping head thing paid off around Christmas. People on my route thought I was a mental case and tipped me heavily to go away.

Even my third-grade teacher got a knit hat. It was a bribe due to my math troubles. Educational experts referred to my condition as "stinking" or "not being very good with numbers." In any case, the knit hat did the trick: I made it to fourth grade. From there my educational progress soared, ending with graduation in the lowest third of my high school class.

In the meantime, Mom moved back to hospital duty on the North Side, becoming chief nurse in a Coronary Care Unit. This was very stressful work, but I think we needed the extra money. Mom slacked off on knitting and smoked more Kools as our family headed into Eighteen Months Without Luck.

In June of 1971, Tim was in college, Mary Pat in high school, and I was in limbo between high school and the rest of my life.

Dad was contemplating taking a postmaster's job out in McHenry County. Then the McCann fortunes—never stellar—did a full gainer off Fate's high dive. Over the next year and a half:

- Dad suffered a heart attack and had to retire from the post office.
- Mary Pat broke her arm in a traffic accident, was hospitalized for mononucleosis, then, with Dad onboard, got in another car wreck.
- Tim broke his wrist playing softball.
- Now a Marine military policeman, I got shot chasing a crazed sentry on Okinawa.
- Mom slipped in an icy parking lot and broke her hip. Her nursing days were finished.

Had a plague of locusts shown up, it would have descended *only on our house* and devoured the zoysia grass and our ancestral lawn gnomes.

Each member of the family dealt with misfortune in his or her own way. (I spent lots of money chasing cute barmaids. Of course, I did that when things were good, so it clearly worked for different moods.) As our sundry injuries healed, Mom dove into knitting with a renewed will. Laid up for a long time, she branched out into intricate patterns. By the late '70s, Mom was at her knitting zenith, crafting the whole family cable-knit Aran fisherman's sweaters. They were truly magnificent.

Aran is a rocky island off the Irish coast. There men carve out a precarious existence, fishing a cold, unforgiving sea in small wooden boats. The women stay home, knit warm sweaters, and engage in currency speculation and offshore banking. (This odd social arrangement has never been adequately explained.)

The Aran sweaters tell stories, much like the tartans of the Scots or the bowling shirts of the Midwest. The sweater's stitches mean different things: The Trinity Stitch baubles, which stick out like little golf balls, represent floats on the nets. The interlaced cables stand for the cables and ropes of the boats. The fishnet filler panels, of course, represent the obvious—government fish subsidies.

Families or villages would have their own sweater pattern that might tell a story about a particular family or region. The McCanns and Fieldings had no pattern that I know of. We were an inland people, less concerned with cresting waves and more interested in sprinting over the peat away from Vikings. We could take or leave fish, but we preferred having a hedge nearby to hide our pigs from the taxman.

Needle Notes

Do the little plastic markers bother your fingers? If so, make your own soft markers with leftover yarn of a different color. They're easy to see and gentler on your hands.

All that aside, our family sorely needed warm sweaters. During the late '70s, the Midwest experienced several exceptionally cold winters. (Given local standards, that's really saying something.) Mary Pat was then at Western Illinois University, where there is nothing to block the wind but corn and good intentions. Tim and I worked outside for the Skokie Post Office. We would stagger off the clock to the nearest bar with rime-covered mufflers and weary eyes, looking like survivors of the Shackleton expedition. Thanks to Mom's acrylic cable knits, though, the McCann youth were cold but not frozen—a fine but critical distinction.

But sweaters couldn't help Mom and Dad. Her hip and his bum heart weren't up to any more Chicago winters. So in 1977 they moved to Eureka Springs, Arkansas. Way up in the Ozark Mountains, this little town was famed for its Passion Play, old hippies, and a high proportion of Chicagoland retirees. Dad joined the Elks and Mom hooked up with a group of women, many of them knitters. They began meeting at my parents' house on Tuesday nights. First they would pray for their families, then they'd knit and drink tea with wild abandon. It was the start of the Last Great Knitting Boom.

Mom became a knitting machine. She knit baby sweaters and caps for friends and relatives, and more hats and sweaters for the family. She hooked afghans until soon every couch and chair in the house had a colorful crocheted backing. Nothing seemed beyond her skill. Mom even knit me a leisure suit and a lounging toga. (I can't swear that I'm remembering the last two items correctly. I took a trip to Puerto Rico around then, toured the Bacardi factory, and bought a lot of odd duty-free stuff.)

As Mom's knitting output increased, the family slowly unwound. Mary Pat and I left Tim and his new wife behind to mind the snow. I moved to Los Angeles in 1979, and Mary Pat moved to Phoenix in 1980. Dad died two years later. In fairness, it had nothing to do with my sister moving to Arizona—he never had an unkind word for the state. His bad heart finally clocked out.

After decades of butting heads with the Old Man, Mom missed the aggravation. Time and space were splitting her away from the family. The kids were scattered all over the country. Of her five siblings, only a brother in New Zealand remained. Mom had a granddaughter now (Tim's) and knitted the new baby some hats and clothes. But she was lonely and wanted to be with Dad. At some point, Mom bought a lot of wool and made travel plans.

Her farewell tour launched in early 1984. Mom swept the

country, visiting all family members and branches, including me in Los Angeles. I was writing and appearing in a series of independent videos that would one day rocket me all the way to the edge of the entertainment industry. It was at that time that Mom brought me the buff-colored turtleneck—The Big Sweater. A wool turtleneck for L.A. winters? These are children's winters out here. But I thanked Mom and took her to Mann's Chinese Theater to see movie star footprints. She found Jeanette Macdonald and Clark Gable and was happier than I'd seen her in a while. And that made me happy.

Mom died that fall from peritonitis. Her system tanked from massive infection. She went into a coma and was gone within a few days. Somehow it seemed Mom had struck a deal with the Great Knitter of All Things. One last family visit, then call it a wrap. The Big Sweater was the last thing she'd knit me and thus it was fat with wool and love.

Mary Pat and I held a farewell session for Mom's Tuesday night chums. It was a quiet sentimental evening, with the women sharing stories about our mother. We invited them to take the afghans Mom had hung over the chairs. This they did on their way out the door, bundling the afghans against the mist as they left in ones and twos, disappearing into the chilly night.

I guess the Big Sweater stands for many things. A reminder of a family's past, woven in stitch and memory; a handy garment to wear if you're going out to smother pipe bombs; or a simple memento of a mother's love. In any case, I'd like to say "Thanks again, Mom" for knitting that sweater. And if it were proper, I would thank the sweater for reminding me of Mom. But I don't talk to my clothes, no matter who made them. I have enough troubles.

John P. McCann

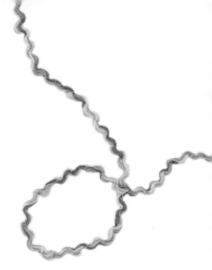

knitted

My mother picks me up after school, after the embroidery class. She turns around from the front seat to look at me closely as I crawl into the station wagon. Why have you been crying? she asks. I don't tell her that I couldn't get the thread through the eye of the needle. I don't tell her I was ashamed to ask for help, so I spent the entire hour pretending to embroider, the empty needle jabbing in and out of the taut muslin, my head down, desperately avoiding the teacher's eye. My friend, Jana, riding beside me in the back, gleefully pipes up to say: She was scared! Of embroidery class! And I shoot her a look that says, all too clearly, traitor. She shrinks back and surreptitiously fingers her own embroidered sampler, still stretched inside its wooden ring, the stitches tiny and perfect. To my mother I mumble only that I don't want to go back, and by this I mean I don't want to go back to any of the after-school offerings: not to the embroidery or the candle-making or the batik. Not to the karate or the tap dance or the synchronized swim. My mother lights a cigarette and pulls away from the curb, steering with one hand. It seems to take a long time before the first pull of smoke exhales in an elaborate sigh. Fine, she says. Whatever you say.

I know her eyes are watching me in the rearview mirror, but I turn to look out the window instead, to see my neighborhood go by in not-quite-a-blur. There's the high wooden fence that holds back the frantic Dobermans, and there's the dangerous patch of sidewalk where the palm trees have upended slabs of concrete. There's the house where Harlan lives, the boy who once spit on me when his friends egged him on to give me a kiss, and there's the Steinberg house where my friend Stacy has white carpet that could so easily be soiled. There's so much to be afraid of, and nothing to be afraid of, and the embroidery was supposed to take my mind off all this, to give me something to think about besides the knots in my stomach and the headache that always hovers behind my eyes. My mother takes another long drag off her cigarette, makes the wide, slow turn onto Mayall, then the quick almost-swerve onto Amestoy. She jabs the cigarette out in the ashtray and turns off the engine. Before she can say anything, Jana and I squiggle out of the car and into the house.

My mother has other things on her mind beside my lack of interest in extracurricular activities. My grandma Bea is coming for a visit. We live three thousand miles away from all of my grandparents, just about as far as one can get, and in my house grandparents are guests, guests we need to clean up for and scrub the oven and get rid of all the nonkosher *traif* foods, like bacon and the thinly sliced ham we put on our sandwiches. My mother, during these pre-grandparent-visit phases, goes around tight-lipped, a cigarette always burning in the ashtray. I hear my father say to her, not unkindly: *What are you afraid of?* And there's nothing to reply, and all I can do is picture my mother shaking her head as she irons the sheets. Already I understand this particular brand of silence: that sometimes you can't put into words what it is you fear, and so all you can do is fear it.

When my grandmother finally arrives, it's apparent there's no cause for alarm. Sure, her ankles are a little bloated and her face is so wrinkled that when she smiles it can be hard to see her eyes. And she has flesh-colored stockings that must be hung on the shower rod, and she won't allow me to brush my hair in the kitchen— *that's one thing I know,* she admonishes, *no hair in the kitchen,* as she removes my bedraggled brush to the bathroom. But she smiles a lot and smells of lavender, and her hands, though already gnarled with impending arthritis, are soft with talcum. She often cups my face in those hands, the palm curved to cradle my chin, and when she does I don't wiggle away but instead sink into that resilient skin.

I hear my mother tell Grandma Bea about the embroidery debacle, and one day Grandma Bea pats the couch and asks me to sit next to her as she knits. So I do, and before long my grandmother's put the long needles in my hands and she's showing me how to knit, the continental way. She holds my hands in hers, guiding the blunt point of the needle under the stitch, around the yarn, pulling it back through, slipping it off. At first I lose a few stitches, and my stomach twists up, but we just keep going and before long I find myself knitting on my own, my grandmother's hands gone, really knitting, and it seems easy—not like the embroidery with its sharp points and slippery thread, not like tap dance, where it's so easy to lose your place and be the fool. There are moments, even, when the yarn seems to be knitting itself, and I can feel the knots in my stomach loosen as I keep knitting, over and over as the pattern insists, in hieroglyphics:

K1, P1, K1, P1—a cadence that becomes the rhythm of my breath, calm, steady, the world aligning itself to this design. A *scarf*, my grandmother says, *for the winter*. Winter's a long way away, but this nascent garment promises that the future exists, inevitable and benign.

As I knit I have no idea—my fingers move and the yarn slides through my knuckles, and the pattern emerges, the new cloth dangles from my needle, as if all along the wool held in its fibers this particular arrangement of useful knots and holes. All along it wanted to please, to be put against the face of someone loved: a child, or a mother, or a man. The tips of my needles whisper and touch; they dip and twist and bow to one another, like the necks of large birds, courting.

ༀༀༀ

Years later, I'm in graduate school in Salt Lake City and I need something, anything, to distract me from my impending oral exams. So I take private knitting lessons at the Black Sheep, from a young man with dreadlocks who smells faintly of garlic. Though it's spring and warm, he wears a bulky hand-knit sweater in shades of ivory and brown. It's awkward at first—he makes me use big wooden needles and a thick caramel wool—but soon enough the familiar gestures of knitting take over and I have in my hands a sampler square, with miniature cables and a perfect little seed stitch running along the sides.

During this spring I'll knit vests on round needles, a pattern that requires no sewing and no fussing with sleeves. I'll find I have a preference for pure cotton yarn; though it tends to separate, the colors are luscious—rich silvers, deep charcoals, bright fuchsia—and I like the smooth, tight stitches I can achieve. I knit nothing for myself: only a vest for my mother, a vest for my friend Amy (who started knitting with me and gave up after the first few rows; I take over her needles as if I'm an expert), a baby sweater in rose cotton for my new niece. I knit during the NBA playoffs—the Jazz are good that year, "Stockton-to-Malone" the mantra of Hot Rod Hundley, his voice in my ear as I sit in front of the television, glancing up now and again at just the right moment to see the fast breaks and the slam dunks. And I'm able to measure my progress against that winning season, though the Jazz will lose at crunch time, beating their heads against the unbeatable Michael Jordan. I offer up my lumpy creations, with all their imperfections (a puckered collar, a curling hem), and always the recipients exclaim their pleasure, running their hands along the fabric and cooing.

I knit in between my four-hour stints at the library, where I read hard, taking notes, trying to absorb DeQuincey and Henry Adams, trying to find my way into Marcus Aurelius and Montaigne. After a while my hands ache for the needles, and I get home and knit furiously while listening to *All Things Considered* or *Selected Shorts*. My mother gives me patterns for lacy dishcloths, small things that take practically no time. I need something I can finish quickly, something that will give me satisfaction but keep me absorbed as the pattern emerges. I like best the Diamond, with all its yarn-overs and slipped stitches, the pattern like another language in which I'm naturally fluent: *YO, P3, K2, Sl1, K1, PSSO*. I'm supposed to be learning French for my translation exam, and I muse on the idea of asking if I can fulfill the requirement by knitting someone a scarf instead.

There's so much to learn. I take lessons in Zen meditation at the local Buddhist temple (the monks wear black, and bow at every opportunity), and I recognize in the repetitive gestures of knitting the steady attention I feel in the zendo, the way the mind, given the opportunity, will circle its way down to a single point of focus. I knit, and I breathe, and the anxiety that always lurks in my belly, that unproductive knot, starts to come undone. I begin to wonder if all fear is really a fear of time passing, the way time slithers away, out of control. Knitting turns time into something that can be measured, shaped into something tactile, with heft and beauty and usefulness. I knit and I knit without looking, so that when the time comes I can know it whole for the first time. Half-done, the other half of the cloth seems already to exist—there, at the curved rim of my needle.

As I knit, I conjoin, invisibly, the strands of all the sentences I've been reading—in English and in French—all the knowledge I've been trying to gain. I wake up on the morning of my oral exams strangely calm, and I bring in Dutch irises and pastries for my committee, not as a bribe so much as an offering, a sacrifice. I take my exams, all of them, and pass with flying colors; they say I know my literature, my French, my writing, well enough to be certified as a Doctor in these things. But what I think I know best is how to sit with time in my hands, to watch time passing, stitch by stitch. I know how to live with imperfection, how to smooth down the pulled stitches and ungraceful knots. I know best how to surrender to mistakes, and what it takes to correct them; how to unravel all you've done to get to the heart of the problem and start over again.

༄༅༄༅

These days I have a print of Vermeer's *The Lacemaker* hanging on my office wall. In this painting we can't really discern the Lacemaker's face full-on; she's too busy gazing down at the work of her hands. Even if we were to call her name, the Lacemaker would not stir, too involved with the delicate task before her. This young woman, I surmise, is not really beautiful—her nose is too large, her cheeks too wide, her forehead broad, and the hair that escapes from her braided bun looks to be a mousy brown—but what makes her gorgeous is the gentle tilt of her eyelids, the faint smile, the connection between that smile and the precise arrangement of her fingers holding her bobbins. Vermeer, of course, illuminates that plain face with a light that makes her saintly, and the lace collar at her neck reflects that light back to the viewer so intensely it almost blinds. In the foreground Vermeer has painted cascades of silk thread loose from their cushioned box, and next to them, a modest book that could be a Bible. This work, of course, is religious work, and requires the same amount of devotion and selflessness. If she did look up from her threads at this moment, I know the Lacemaker's eyes would brim with tears.

I thought I was drawn to this painting because I saw in the woman's labor my own work as a writer, and I wanted to achieve that same kind of loving concentration with words as this woman does with her bobbins of silk thread. But what I see now is that the Lacemaker is really the quintessence of mindfulness, and when I look at her I'm ushered into the same state of focus as when I meditate on the tiny brass statues of the Buddha in my meditation room. She embodies a central tenet of Buddhist texts: "To study the self is to forget the self. To forget the self is to be actualized by myriad things. . . ." With the Lacemaker, and with my grandmother while knitting, I think their selves grew fluid, the boundaries between their bodies and the bodies of others—between their hands and the work that moved through them—became mere illusion.

I still have a fisherman's sweater my Grandma Bea knit for me at least twenty years ago, in creamy synthetic wool, with the classic cables and seed stitches running all along the torso and down the sleeves. It's pilled and frayed, impossible to clean, but it somehow still fits me no matter how much time has passed. Every few years I get it down from its shelf and pull it over my head. I remember it as being scratchy, but when I put it on I find it's not really abrasive at all, just soft and resilient, heavily textured, the color still luscious, almost glowing. I can see my grandmother's fingertips, how they held knitting needles so lightly it seemed they weren't being held at all, just guided by an ephemeral touch that could turn string into sweater, afghan, scarf. She had the same relaxed, reverent concentration on her face as Vermeer's Lacemaker, that same beatific smile at work finely done.

"Knitting is cosmic thinking."
—RUDOLF STEINER

Though I never wear it for more than a few minutes at a time, the sweater's survived a hundred moves, never quite making it into the Goodwill bag; at the last minute I always pull it out, horrified, as if I've nearly discarded my grandmother's body. I put it back on a shelf, where it will sit until the next time I move, my version of a funeral urn.

The sweater is one of many things that endures. Vermeer's Lacemaker will abide, her fingers forever held captive by silk bobbins; the knowledge I pieced together from books will endure, as will my smattering of French, as will the writing I labor over, the small passages I hope might persist in a reader's mind long after I've put down the pen. And the past endures: my grandmother's soft palms, or that young girl stitching and stitching in embroidery class, the empty needle swooping into the muslin.

I imagine my grandmother's sweater covering my frail torso when I'm old, sitting on some porch in sweater weather, calm, no longer with any fear of the future because the future has already arrived. In my hands I'll hold the knitting needles, but will it matter if I have any yarn? Perhaps, as a young girl in embroidery class, I had it right all along: It didn't matter if I threaded my needle or not, because it was the practice of stitching that mattered, the steady tempo of my hands. Maybe, by that time, I'll need only the dipping and clicking, needles making their own patterns of the air. Like the embodiment of a Zen koan, I'll keep knitting away: Thread, no thread, yarn, no yarn—what kind of garment can one weave with memory?

Brenda Miller

Two: Check Your Gauge

"What a pity that you were not born a boy so that you
could be good for something. Run into the house, child,
and go to knitting."

—FRANCES D. GAGE

We knit to show our love, and sometimes, to claim the
physical bodies of those we love. If only I make him this
sweater, the thinking goes, I'll knit into place a perfect future for us,
I'll smooth over the rough patches of our couplehood with wool. I'll
create something better than the reality of what already exists.

There's a longstanding bit of advice from knitters I've
often heard. A woman should never knit a sweater for her
boyfriend, it's rumored, because that's the way to destroy
the nascent love. It's the kiss of death. Rather, one should
hold off until there's an engagement ring at the least, or
better yet, a marriage certificate to ensure you'll be around
to see that beloved sweater over the
Not that that's any real guarantee. Still,

it's amazing how many knitters claim failed relationships after prematurely knitting a sweater.

In this chapter's first essay, Rebecca Kuder reminds us that, just as it's seldom wise to make a sweater without first checking your gauge, it likewise can be problematic to enter a love affair with a partner whose "gauge" is unlike your own. You can't smooth over a bad fit easily.

With love, sweater-making, and just about anything else we do, checking our gauge—seeing where and how things will come together and verifying the fit beforehand—often seems like an extra unnecessary step. But it can go a long way in avoiding broken hearts, a poor fit, and wasted time. As they say in the world of carpentry, measure twice, cut once.

Remember: check your gauge.

fit

In my hand is a small ball of wool yarn. Irregular, lighter than the real indigo dye used in my college fiber arts class, this wool has been with me for fifteen years. A remnant, left over from the last sweater I knit for someone other than myself. I wrote him a Danish blue love letter in yarn, sent it, and the next year, regretted it.

Knitting calls forth something primal—to keep those I care about warm and protected. Knitting sweaters for boyfriends, beyond the quiet glory of giving handmade gifts, can also punctuate a sense of possessiveness and desire for permanence. I knit, I tie myself to another person, I wrap him in a web of knots. Wearing what I've made for him, he becomes visibly more "mine." In my life, this innocent yearning to own a loved one has often become tangled, a knotted mess of nubby yarn.

My mother taught me to knit when I was in high school. She showed me how to knit 3 inches, and then stop, check my gauge, and make sure those inches had the proper number of stitches indicated in the pattern so my creations would grow to the right size, and would not be distorted. But I was always impatient. Checking my gauge was too fussy. Close enough seemed close enough for me— a half inch here or there, so what? I thought I could manage without that methodical preparation, depending on well-timed improvisation and charm to get me out of various jams. The free-form approach didn't always work, not in life or in knitting. I would rush into love, before thought, not evaluating the fit. I would do what I could to make it work. I would overlook the loose-fitting gaps, or the overly constraining tightness. If I held my breath, or stood up taller, or smiled and kept quiet, no one would notice the saggy sweater.

I began with scarves.

Scarves were easy: lap back and forth, like swimming, and it didn't matter if they fit. If a scarf warmed the intended neck, it was a success. If a scarf wound around a neck three times instead of once, at least it met the basic human need for warmth. I knit scarves for friends; I recall one synthetic baby-blue scarf, made for a spindly blond boy, its color an attempt to match his eyes. Eventually I graduated from scarves and knit a maroon sweater vest for my father. It was long. Excessively long. He said he liked it: in addition to his torso, it warmed his butt.

When I was a senior in high school, I fell in love with a soulful junior who played guitar. We determined that, because we had been childhood playmates, it was destiny, and we would be together forever. We named theoretical children, and we speculated about what they would look like, examining curled photographs of our own tiny faces. I decided to knit him a sweater.

My mother and I went to Martha's Yarn Shop, a small house converted into a store, where floor-to-ceiling shelves overflowed with color, texture, possibilities. Buttery, poetic names like Martifil Soft and Tipperary Tweed whispered and beckoned. Yarn from Scotland, France, Italy, all brought to Ohio for our tactile reverie. Martha had any kind and size of needle a person could imagine, stitch holders, all types of intricate tools, and complicated and so-called simple patterns. Not only a shopkeeper, she also gave advice. You could ask her anything, or you could bring a confounding half-knit cable sweater fragment to her, and she could usually help. Going there with my mother, I felt I had entered some vague yet important subset of femininity, and though I considered knitting to be the act of old ladies, I thought I was making it new, fresh with my young, blushing love.

I chose forest green tweed wool, Irish, with flecks of brown and blue and other bits of color—strong, warm, and expensive. I camped on the couch and knit and knit, and eventually, it was done. I pieced the panels together, sleeve to sleeve, side to side. As was apparent in my father's sweater vest, my mother's perfect gauge was not hereditary. The boy was tall, but the green crew-neck sweater was sized for a giant. He said he loved it anyway, and I took in the sides so it wasn't twice the size it needed to be. The bunchy side seams made him look bulky, but he was so flawlessly in love that he wore it anyway.

I went away to college, and the boy started his senior year. We agreed that we could see other people, and began a torturously slow breakup. Humiliated, after pointlessly and unsuccessfully begging him to stay with me, there was a tendril of myself that yearned to ask him to give back the sweater. But that would be rude. I had made it for him, and besides, what would I do with an altered, giant sweater?

Ever optimistic, at college I found another boyfriend. And another opportunity to knit. He was from Brooklyn, and this time the project was a V-neck, black cotton, which complemented his fair skin and dark hair. I would create the most urban version of the hand-knit sweater. I checked my gauge, and if it was a little off, so what? The black cotton was soft and covered my lap with downy fuzz as I worked. I should have used it for myself: I coveted that yarn. The black V-neck fit a little better than the high school giant's, though it was quite roomy. I still have a photo of him wearing it. But the eventual interpersonal catastrophe hit, clearly my fault this time, and we broke up. The downfall was my impatience. I disregarded the rules of our relationship, our gauge. I was distracted by another man.

The next year, I became entangled with a strawberry-blond-haired soccer player. He had traveled throughout Europe, and he had lived in Denmark, so the natural choice was Danish blue wool. The one lonely fragment I still have now rests softly on my desk. The soccer player came from a family of academics, so this time I would try a cardigan. I found some distressed metal buttons for a bohemian touch. The cardigan fit better than the previous pullovers had, as the soccer player fit better with me. But as with the others—sweaters or men—none exactly flattered. Eventually, after various romantic contortions, he left me for a woman who had my first name, Rebecca. Her last name was Moore. Rebecca Moore. As if I wasn't enough.

It took those years of giving too much for me to decide it was bad luck to knit sweaters for boyfriends. The relationship would end and I would secretly want the sweater

Needle Notes

Learn to check your gauge. Knit up a swatch about 2 inches square, then measure how many stitches are in each inch. Let's say you're getting a stitch and a half. Measure 2 inches' worth and divide it by two, being sure to count the partial stitch amount. (An extra half stitch every inch will throw your final measurements off by a good bit.) If you have too many stitches, decrease your needle size by one and try again. If you have too few, increase the needle size.

back, but not be strong enough to ask. Still, had any of these ill-fitting people really appreciated my work? For years, I fantasized that they were sentimental enough (and still secretly in love with me, despite all the betrayal we had shared), and therefore they must still worship their misshapen sweaters, stashed in the backs of closets, hidden from their probably tall, blonde, and glamorous wives. I decided sweaters were only worth making if you know you'll stay together.

I decided to knit a sweater for myself.

I found a rosy rust merino wool and cotton blend, feathery soft. When I squeezed a skein of the yarn, it collapsed in my hand, airy and seductive, like puff pastry. I knit this mythic stuff into a V-neck using a great new method: all one piece on circular needles. No piecing together, no bunches of meaningless panels languishing, needing final attention at the last stage, when I was the most impatient. Reminding me of my knitting foundations, the epic one-piece sweater was huge ("check your gauge, check your gauge," my mother's advice echoed, too late). However, I liked big floppy things then, and it was roomy, with more drape than bulk, and it was warm and soft and who cared if it was twice as wide as necessary? It was mine.

Years later, I got married. I had been telling my husband for years before our wedding that I couldn't knit him a sweater because it was a possible curse against the relationship. On our wedding day, I gave him a card with a promise that *now* I could safely knit him a sweater. I never got the chance. The marriage didn't last long. Maybe I knew I wouldn't have time to finish. Maybe the boyfriends had ruined something that could have been for my husband. But I should have known that a relationship could end, with or without a sweater.

When I was in college, my mother had shown me a sweater she had knit for my father. It was a deep green-blue wool V-neck, with small, moth-eaten holes in several places. I'm sure with her gauge it must have fit him perfectly at the time. But they had divorced when I was young.

I kept the sweater, and wore it, loving the idea that she had made it for him, and I even cherished its holes. What is this urge for us to warm those we love, this primal need to comfort, protect, and own? Yet it's no assurance of permanence, only an ideal, because we can never be sure the other person wants our love at all.

So instead of a sweater, for my husband I spun endless trips to the emergency room for migraines and mania, and I gave him whatever of my own Rebecca yarn that I could, as much as he needed; frantic, I reeled it out faster and faster, but the snarled, matted, twisted pile made nothing and wasn't enough to keep him warm.

ᔕᔕᔕ

I recently became engaged again. He's from Texas, and he rarely wears sweaters. I think he doesn't have any he likes particularly well. From our early days, I knew he was likely to stay. Because I am so sure of him, I have been tempted to knit him a sweater. My superstition about sweaters is still intact, but I did knit him a scarf, soft green cotton, useful, washable, to keep his warm-weather-born neck toasty during Ohio winters. I decided to make the scarf in broad ribbing, so it would hang nicely. I cast on 60 or 80 stitches and began my needle laps, back and forth, and as it grew, it got heavier and heavier. I should have stopped, torn it out, started over with a narrower width, fewer stitches. I hadn't considered that the ribbing would double its weight. The scarf ended up twice as wide and much heavier than it needed to be.

Maybe it was trying to be a sweater.

This romantic yet practical man wore the green albatross several times, then gently told me that the scarf was too wide, too big. Repeating my own pattern—impatience—I over-knit. My eagerness to warm overwhelmed my history of ill fit. And while he appreciated the gesture, the scarf languishes in the closet, draped over a sturdy hanger. And yet, because he is who he is, and although I am still who I am, for him, I would check my gauge, and knit him a new scarf, or ten sweaters, until something fits.

Rebecca Margaret Kuder

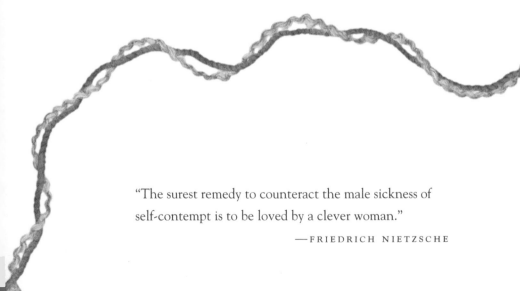

"The surest remedy to counteract the male sickness of self-contempt is to be loved by a clever woman."

—FRIEDRICH NIETZSCHE

the secret of perfect tension

Back when Harlem had front
porches and the city sat
in the steamed tar of summer
she learned to knit.

The city sat
out. Her feet dangled over the bug
dusted floor. Nana took orders
for hand-pleated lamps that paid the grocer

Dangled over the bug-dusted floor,
her finger held straight, stiff.
The yarn spooled from skein to needle
never stopped or snagged or pulled.

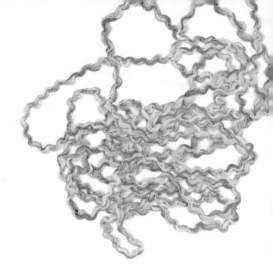

Held straight, stiff, the yarn,
Each stitch identical,
to the next as if factory formed.
She learned cable knit.

Each stitch identical,
twisted susan and the old Man
lurched home from Kelsey's pub
up the scorched rungs of the fire

escape. And the old Man lurched home.
She perched a rhythmic click, clicking—
single ball of cheap red yarn.
Her finger straight and still.

Kathleen Lohr

crafty

I am not a particularly crafty person. I don't decoupage. I've never handpainted anything. Using a glue gun is as foreign to me as using a machine gun. But knitting I can do. It's vaguely creative, but really, all you do is follow a pattern. Sure, you can design your own sweaters, but for me, knitting is picking a yarn or two, leafing through books or magazines for a simple pattern, and following said pattern to the letter. It's kind of like paint-by-numbers with a hefty price tag.

I learned to knit while pregnant with twins, partially out of a need to nest, but mostly out of a desire to stave off the mind-numbing boredom I anticipated suffering during my inevitable bed rest. Bed rest was boring, but it also prepared me for a radical life change. Rather than abruptly switching gears from frenetic freelance television writer and producer to frantic mother of two, I had two months of bed rest as a rest stop on the road to motherhood.

Even with the medically sanctioned transition built in, motherhood took a lot of getting used to. Suddenly, I wasn't a career woman—I was a walking milk machine, chained to two hungry mouths (which were attached to two babies in hand-knit clothes). I could no longer lounge in bed in the morning. Sunday's paper had to wait until Wednesday, when I finally decided I was never going to read it and threw it out. I grew proficient at doing everything with one hand, so that the other could hold a baby. My social life changed, my priorities changed, and my figure—well, let's not even go there. But none of this was shocking. I'd expected those changes. I'd chosen them. Sure, my social circle was different, but it was easy to find other new moms to talk to, other frazzled parents looking for kindred souls. I settled into my new life, and started knitting again. But if the ramifications of becoming a mother were expected, the dire social and sexual repercussions of becoming a knitter were not.

Knitting, according to the media and the crowds at my local knitting shop, has enjoyed a resurgence lately. Young women are knitting themselves big chunky sweaters and slinky little tank tops, and young moms are eschewing $250 hand-knit baby sweaters in boutiques to spend $300 and countless hours knitting their own mini-masterpieces. Even so, there's a stereotype about knitters. Old ladies knit. Spinsters knit. And expectant mothers knit. When I became a knitter I entered this triumvirate. With each stitch, I knit away my sensuality and crafted myself into a drool-wiping, poop-cleaning, spit-up-covered Mommy with the same sexual appeal as the old ladies and spinsters whose sisterhood I had joined.

How do I know this? Several weeks ago, I was riding the subway when a good-looking man smiled at me and took the seat next to mine. As a mother of two-year-old twins, I feel lucky when men don't recoil in horror from my disheveled hair and food-stained clothes, so this small smile translated into a big ego boost for me. Were I still single, I would have been planning our honeymoon by the next stop. But then I pulled out my knitting needles. Mr. Attractive looked at me with abject disgust. "Jesus Christ," he exploded, and dramatically harrumphed himself to the other side of the subway car, plunking himself down next to a presumably nonknitting man.

Perhaps he thought the knitting needles were weapons, and were the train to come to a sudden stop, I would stab him in the jugular, and he would get blood stains on his Armani tie. A male friend of mind suggested that I had "shattered the poor guy's image" of me. B.K.N. (Before Knitting Needles) I was a babe, a woman of style, daringly braving the subway's toxic fumes and even more toxic passengers. A.K.N. (After Knitting Needles) I was a Knitter: a grandmotherly spinster expecting twins while doddering around my cat-filled house in a tattered housedress and hip-high underwear. (His theory was subsequently proven when a client of mine walked into my edit room to find me knitting and blurted out "Hey, whatever happened to that sexy babe I used to know?" Ouch.)

It's no surprise to learn that this equation is correct: Sleep deprivation + No time for the gym − Privacy = Declined sexual activity and desire.

But since when does being crafty make someone undesirable? Granted, Martha Stewart isn't exactly a sexual icon, but I think that's more due to a certain WASP-y *froideur* than to her proclivity for glue guns and "good things." But from what I can tell, knitting, not mothering, has changed my sexuality, or at least the perception of it.

Picture this: My husband and I are lying in bed at night after mealtime, bath time, story time, and bedtime are complete. I'm knitting. He languidly reaches across to caress me lovingly and *ugh*! My knitting needle stabs him in the chest leaving my children fatherless and me with a whole lot of bloody bedding to clean. Unless you're extremely kinky, this is not a romantic scene.

But let's say my hobby was—oh, I don't know—long jumping. Then the scene would play out quite differently: My husband lies in bed after my incredibly toned physique has made it possible for me to complete mealtime, bath time, and all those other "times" in one fell swoop. He looks at me as I cross the room, and without missing a beat, I long-jump over the dirty laundry, onto the bed, and into his arms.

See? Long jumping = sexy. Knitting = deadly.

Knitting has changed my social appeal, too. A few months ago, I was sitting in a café. A group of single women admired my shoes, which of course sparked conversation. (Ah, shoes! The only thing I can still wear in a size six!) We talked about restaurants, shoes, politics, shoes. I showed them pictures of my kids. They oohed. They aahed. I said something witty and self-deprecating. We laughed. I ordered another chai latte. Then I took out my knitting. The women all pretended to be impressed by my skill and dedication. But the conversation died. Perhaps they feared that knitting was contagious. Conversing with me might lead them, too, to feel the urge to knit and thereby lose their sensual identities. Being a mother was fine. Being a knitting mother was not.

Even without the knitting, though, I didn't really fit in with those women. I don't really know where I fit in anymore. I have my husband, my family, a few close friends, but those early days of instant sisterhood between new mothers have waned, a casualty of the stresses of mothering toddlers. Motherhood has forced me to craft a whole new vision of myself. Where I used to be eminently capable, I'm now permanently overwhelmed. Where I once kept up on the latest restaurants, I now keep mac and cheese in the cupboard. And while I used to track my success in dollars earned, I now know I'm doing well when I earn thank-yous, pleases, and I-love-yous from two two-year-olds. Invaluable, yes, but unquantifiable. What is my worth now? The threads of my life have become tangled.

Working part-time only complicates matters. Am I a mother or a careerist? Is motherhood affecting my work, or working affecting the quality of my mothering? I wonder if stay-at-home moms lose it and yell at their kids, if they have time to cook real meals and keep their floors clean. I have trouble finding myself in this quagmire of questions. The only things I can hold on to are my two two-year-olds' hands.

But then I put my toddlers in their coordinated red-white-and-blue jumpers that I knit on subways and buses and during rare downtime late at night, and I know who I am. I'm a proud mother. I'm a capable woman. So there are dust bunnies under the bed. There are piles of pictures waiting to be put into albums. There are days I wish for time alone, wish my kids would stop screaming, or wish I could order in instead of making dinner. I even leave my children sometimes and go to work. But I do knit. Look, there they are, matching sweaters, slightly lumpy, maybe, but concrete, quantifiable knitwear. Made by me.

Knitting lets me interweave my life at work with my life at home. I bring my knitting to freelance jobs, and in the inevitable downtime on set I knit little sweaters and vests and dresses. I knit to keep a connection to my babies even while I'm working. I knit to tie myself to them with a not-so-invisible thread. I knit so that when some perfect-looking mother who surely never yells at her kids, or feeds them takeout, or even knows what a dust bunny is, asks me wherever did I get those beautiful baby sweaters, I can answer proudly: "I made them myself." Turns out I'm pretty crafty after all. Crafty and damn proud of it.

Nancy Rabinowitz

"I never worry about running out of yarn and mixing dye lots, and I often combine all sorts of yarns in the same garment."

—KAFFE FASSETT, *Glorious Knits*

mawk

❧ Her name was Mary, but when her grandson was three he decided that since he had two grandmothers, he would call this one Mawk. No one knew why he picked this particular name, but from then on everyone called her Mawk.

She was the true matriarch of the family. A small woman who was definitely in charge. When I married my husband, his grandmother Mawk was in her sixties. She had survived a cancer operation, even though the doctors gave little hope that she would.

She worked nights as a private duty nurse. And during the night when not attending her patients she knitted. In fact, I very seldom saw her when she wasn't knitting. Click, click, click, you always knew where to find her by the sound of the knitting needles. She had several grandchildren, but my husband was her favorite. It was obvious from the start that she didn't like me. However, I think it would have been the same no matter whom he married. She was cold and aloof when I entered the house, and she didn't have much to say unless it was a sarcastic remark.

Every year at Christmas, Mawk gave gifts to her family that she had knitted. Sweaters, socks, scarves, etc. My gift from her every year was bath powder. Then one by one as the family opened them, she made comments. "I used blue yarn for you because you have such beautiful blue eyes." "I thought you would like a red scarf to go with the sweater I gave you." And so on and so forth.

When I was pregnant with my first child, she knitted an afghan for the baby. I went out of my way to show my appreciation, thanking her profusely. She stiffened her little bony body, looked at me over her glasses and said, "I'm glad you appreciate the work involved. I hope you launder it properly."

I was brought up to respect my elders, but it was all I could do to keep my mouth shut. I wanted to tell her what I thought. Mawk was spoiled and doted on by her family. She said whatever she wanted. No one dared to confront her.

When I had my second child, she knitted a beautiful sweater, hat, and booties for the baby. We were living out of town at the time, but I showed my appreciation by sending her a thank-you note. Later I had a call from her daughter. During the course of our conversation she got around to asking if I would please write and thank Mawk for the baby gift. She'd told the family that I had not thanked her. I didn't bother sending a second note.

One cold winter night, the family had gathered together at an aunt's house and someone suggested making waffles. Mawk was her usual charming self, and turned to ask me if I ever fixed waffles for my family. I told her no. She straightened in her chair, and with a smirk on her face asked, "Why, is it too much trouble?" That was all it took; I finally had had enough. I stayed as calm as possible, and I told her that I didn't like her remark; in fact, I hadn't liked many of her remarks over the years, and I wasn't going to visit her any more if it continued. The room was quiet; no one moved. I didn't know what to expect. Mawk had her lips pursed and was squinting at me. Looking around the room I detected little smiles on some of the faces. And then from across the room in a booming voice, Uncle Charlie said, "Well, let's cook the waffles; I'm hungry." Surprisingly, there were no sarcastic remarks directed my way the rest of the evening.

I didn't know how my husband would react to what had occurred. On the way home I told him I was sorry about what happened. His response was that Mawk had been asking for it, and he knew that it was just a matter of time before I told her how I felt about her rudeness.

The next year at Christmas when Mawk handed her gifts to the family, I didn't get the usual gift of bath powder. Instead I got a beautiful white sweater that was decorated with a stripe of blue angora yarn. In my opinion it was the prettiest sweater that she knitted that year. I was overwhelmed, and I gave her a big hug. She had tears in her eyes, and I knew she was truly sorry that she had not been nice to me throughout the years. But that day all was forgiven.

Mawk worked as a nurse until she was seventy-five years old. She continued to knit until the age of ninety-seven after falling and breaking her hip. Throughout the years I received many wonderful knitted gifts from Mawk. But my most treasured one was the white sweater with the blue angora trim.

E. M. Ritt

GAUGE-FREE SCARF

If gauge is your downfall, try garments that will work despite gauge until you get it down. Here's a scarf pattern that's hard to mess up.

Choose yarn and needle sizes you like, keeping in mind that the thicker the yarn, the bulkier the scarf; and the fatter the needles, the more space between each stitch. Slender yarn knit on thin needles will take a long time to knit up and will produce a finely textured scarf, while chunky yarn on fat needles will quickly produce a stout, plump scarf.

Cast on stitches until you have nearly the width you desire. Make it a bit narrower for the cast-on row because the scarf will thicken up a bit as you work.

Knit every row until you reach the right length or you run out of yarn.

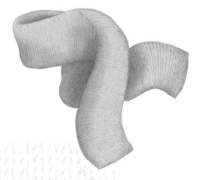

Needle Notes

Are you knitting a scarf or afghan in stockinette stitch and finding that the curling of the knitted fabric isn't what you want? Switch to garter stitch—knit every row—and the curling will be a thing of the past. Or, you can add a border in ribbing or stockinette to keep things flat.

53

the k1, p2 profile

⊗ Sometimes I worry that my life is boring. I dance. I knit. I have a desk job sitting in front of a computer, and I've been cubicle-bound at various companies for sixteen years. It doesn't look good on paper.

I know a woman who used to be a stockbroker and also owner of a financial services company that she sold at the height of the dot-com boom. Then she divorced her husband, who had storied Hollywood connections; set up a dance studio teaching tango in Los Angeles; bought a Mercedes; and cut a CD of her folk guitar stylings with a three-man alternative rock combo. All in less time than it took me to teach myself continental-style knitting and three-needle bind-off.

In my worst moments I imagine a dinner party that goes something like this: The folk stylings CD gets passed around. On the CD cover she is wearing a western-style jacket done in woven stitch, and I ask her, "Hey, did you knit this? It looks like something from *Vogue Knitting*, fall issue, 1992." She looks at me blankly. "Do you knit?" The entire table turns to me. I nod yes. There is a giant pause. I am supposed to supply an earth-shattering punch line. And then someone asks Renaissance Woman, "Are you going to do another CD?" Her response is coy; she is busy writing a screenplay and shopping it around to associates of her ex-husband's. I am deflated. No, I didn't design the sweaters on last season's *Gilmore Girls*. I do not have a Web site. It was not me who crocheted the barely-there bikinis in an upcoming episode of some reality TV show, and I do not have items for sale at Anthropologie. This is L.A. If you knit, you'd better knit big. And I don't mean bulky sweaters.

Let me clarify. My life doesn't bore me, it just sounds boring. At parties. Or online in a profile on match.com. What do you do for a living? I'm a technical writer. I write documents that are usually called something like the "MX 4170 User Manual." People who don't know any better sometimes say, "Wow, that must be interesting!" Most of the time I agree, though having to create thousands of variations on "To display the MX 4170's system statistics, enter the system info command" gives me pause. What else about me? I love to salsa dance. That sounds sexy. I put that into my match.com profile. I dance. I write. I knit. Would you like to go out with me?

I didn't explain in my profile that I own an assortment of plastic tubs filled with knitted sweaters and hats and scarves and felted backpacks and an assortment of failed vests. I've made these things over the course of thirty years of knitting (though I have divested myself of most of the early works by now). I guess thirty years gives away something about my age, and I can't claim to have started knitting in the womb. In Psalms, King David says that we are God's knitted work: "You knit me together in my mother's womb" (Ps. 139:13, New International

Version). I live 2,500 miles from my niece Rachel, and one day at age five she woke up and announced that she wanted to knit. God knit into both of us (and my father's mother, too) the desperate desire to create something out of yarn.

Knitting is a big part of my life, but I am afraid to advertise it. I have friends who have known me for years, not realizing that those sweaters I wore last winter were something that I did not purchase from Nordstrom. When they find out, I dump one of the plastic bins on the floor and let them ooh and aah. These are female friends, of course. Some are lucky recipients of my handiwork; I derive a lot of pleasure in seeing them discover that the baby blanket cascading in lovely waves on their parental laps was Made by Jen.

Knitting has a bad reputation, especially with men. Maybe knitting for them is beyond domesticity, a kind of antithesis of sex. It reminds them of mothers or grandmothers, or unmarried aunts holed up in attics on Cape Cod who eventually die alone without secret lovers or hidden histories, just huge stashes of unused yarn. These men have no idea what the completion of a finely executed lace pattern can accomplish; it's a feeling that lasts a long, long time.

In the end, I thought it was more important to begin educating men than to get a date. I edited my profile on match.com to include that I was a voracious knitter, that I consumed yarn and patterns like a fiber corollary of the Cookie Monster.

The men thought it was quaint. Or they didn't comment. They liked my photo, they always said. What about my penchant for independent film? What about walks along the Big Sur coastline? What about my ability to produce one-of-a-kind scarves with two sticks and finely handpainted string? Nada. They liked my photo.

So I got offline, and I got aggressive. I started talking about my knitting in public places, perusing my knitting catalogs while standing at the counter and waiting for the cute Starbucks kid to finish my tall decaf mocha. I talked about knitting at parties with single men. Maybe the words in the air, rather than on the page, would make the knitting sexy. And justify my recent two-hundred-dollar purchase of Colinette yarn off of eBay.

The author, with two children of a friend.

"Knitting? Why would you want to be knitting when you could be dancing?" said a guy at the Derby one night. We met in an East Coast swing class offered before the band started. He was a dancing geek. I was on my way to becoming a dancing geek, dancing two or three times a week like the rest of them. But I'd been a knitting geek for much longer, way before I even knew what to call it. I did not go out with this guy.

Months later at a party in Laguna Beach, a musician named Wayne took me aside to explain why I should eject my short-term boyfriend and get back into the singles scene. The boyfriend was a computer system troubleshooter type, someone whose biggest aspiration was to have enough money at retirement to travel the country in a Winnebago. Wayne asked what I did for fun, since he assumed the boyfriend was not supplying any. I said, "I knit."

"You knit? How boring!"

"Boring!" Maybe it was the wine, a thick, buttery Chardonnay, the kind I don't risk drinking when I'm knitting complicated, charted Aran patterns, but my chest swelled and I spewed, "You don't know about fiber, the wools, cottons, boucles, the million ways to cast on and bind off, two-stranded knitting, double knitting, entrelac, seed stitch, I-cord, backwards crocheted edgings, yarn-overs, and passing the damn slip stitch over!"

"Geez, I had no idea it was so involved," he said.

I almost went out with Wayne.

Knitting can be a stumbling block on the road to coupledom, because it is a fine companion in itself. I have been known to converse for hours with some deliciously soft purple alpaca while curled

The author's nephew shows off his new present.

up in a tank top and shorts in the corner of my ultrasuede sofa with a thousand knitting books and magazines strewn on the coffee table.

But then I met a math teacher in a Lindy Hop class on a sticky Saturday morning in Pasadena.

You can't wear your bulky knitted sweaters to dance class (except as a coat in the mild southern California winter). I usually don't wear my scarves either because I don't want to sweat on them. So I had to blurt out to the math teacher early on that I was a knitter, not just a dancer. He was not fazed. What could he say? He was a math teacher, after all. And he understood delight in accomplishing something with movement—a perfect swing-out in Lindy Hop, a perfect cross-body lead in salsa dance. When I execute a series of perfectly spotted turns on the dance floor, it's kind of like finishing an invisible seam on two knitted pieces of stockinette stitch. Except with knitting you actually have proof that you did it.

I explained to the math teacher the intricacies of gauge and the topology of Aran patterns and Fair Isle colorwork, how they were mathematical. How you desperately needed to know how to measure and calculate to make sure whatever you were knitting would come out the appropriate size. Without math you couldn't resize or modify a pattern or create one of your own. The math teacher wrote a mathematical proof to prove that we should go out on a date; a year later I made him a scarf. I tell him I love him; maybe the scarf is a physical proof of that love.

He's sleeping on my sofa now, his head almost touching a couple of balls of multicolored sock yarn, a handful of double-pointed bamboo knitting needles, and some rosewood crochet hooks from my grandmother angled dangerously near his nose. I'm sitting at my home computer pounding away at a short story or finishing up some procedural material for work ("Press Enter to save your changes"), or maybe I'm writing into the long hours of the night about knitting. My fingers are gliding over the keyboard; there's a rhythmic, soothing clicking, like the sound of knitting needles bringing forth something new.

Jennifer Jameson

Three: Baby Knits

"Everyone knows that by far the happiest and universally enjoyable age of man is the first. What is there about babies which makes us hug and kiss and fondle them, so that even an enemy would give them help at that age?"

—DESIDERIUS ERASMUS

What can compare to the experience of knitting for an expected birth? The nine months of waiting is a time of joyful anticipation. If we're the ones who are pregnant, our only real job is to take care of ourselves, eat well, and get lots of rest. This leaves us, though, with all our myriad dreams, hopes, and expectations floating around, waiting to be turned into something tangible. Knitting can serve that purpose.

If someone else is pregnant, we may want to share the experience, let the mother-to-be know we're with her in her moment of expectation. We can knit our joy into a baby garment and show our love one at a time.

Knitting can celebrate a coming life, but it can also keep our hands and minds busy when worries threaten to overwhelm us. And knitting is a way we can give back to our community, creating hand-knit items for charities like Stitches from the Heart, a nonprofit organization that has provided nearly 100,000 items to maternity departments across the nation over the past four years. The baby cap pattern in this chapter is provided by a Stitches from the Heart volunteer; with it, there's information on how you, too, can knit to make a difference by delighting families whose babies have been born prematurely or with a serious illness.

Expecting a child should be a wonderful, exciting time, but it is often fraught with worry. Knitting gives us something to do with those fears and a way to transform them into blessings.

"the endearing elegance of female friendship" *

It's beautiful. The color is a bright blue, like the trim on my favorite white houses at the seaside. The combination of wool and silk make it soft and weighty. The pattern is richly textured. It has a boatneck and three-quarter sleeves, just like I wanted. I love it, this sweater that my best friend Crystie knitted for me . . . finally.

I almost always preface her name with the phrase "best friend" when I talk about Crystie, even though I have other women in my life who are very dear and important. We met at age eleven and agreed to be best friends when we were thirteen. It would seem a betrayal to bestow that title on anyone who may have arrived belatedly during the last thirty-eight years.

We told each other everything during our tumultuous adolescence, which made negotiating school, boys, and sex much less

* Samuel Johnson

traumatic than it might otherwise have been. The one omission was when Crystie did some heavy petting with George Hernandez that she didn't tell me about until years after for fear of my reaction. She was contrite about the breach in our sworn honesty, and I believe it never happened again.

↬↭↬

Crystie and I were intellectually compatible; we had met in a creative writing class and enjoyed reading the same books and spending weekend nights when we weren't out cruising for boys, reading plays aloud to each other in her basement. We both talked so fast that others had trouble understanding us. Someone once made a tape of one of our conversations. It was unintelligible even to us when it was played back, though at the time we had understood each other perfectly. In the men department we were very different, but it came out even. She, like me, was a little late to date, but with her huge blue eyes, tiny waist, and wild golden hair, she was definitely sexier and more popular with guys. I was tall, dark, and reasonably handsome and tended toward fewer, longer-term relationships. We lost our virginity within a month of each other the summer after high school, more out of a sense of camaraderie with one another than with either of the unsuspecting boys.

In clothes, however, we were of different castes. She

Needle Notes

When knitting for a baby, keep in mind practical things. Choose a yarn that's soft on the skin and easy to wash. An heirloom wool is great for the hope chest, but may be a thorn in the side of any mother who'd like her spitting-up infant to actually wear it. Today there are many brands of natural fibers, including wool and cotton, that are even machine washable. Check them out.

had a great figure and money to spend. I was poor and struggled with my weight. From prepubescence until early middle age, our pattern was to go shopping together—I to watch, her to buy. She dressed up. I dressed down. She could smashingly accessorize every outfit; I wore the same sentimental necklace and ring wherever I went. We shared similar tastes, but my role was as appreciator of her impressive collection.

I accepted this with little resentment in every area but one: hand-knit sweaters. That's because it was the one place where Crystie could have made a difference in my wardrobe. She learned how to knit young and she knitted ever more lovely creations as she got older. But never for me. It pained me that she would knit a sweater for some boyfriend who I knew would be gone in a matter of months while our friendship had endured much longer—decades eventually. So I pressed her. Wasn't her love for me as important as her love for them? Even as girls, we knew better than to turn on one another or break important plans for a mere boy, and the feminism we embraced in college reinforced our notions about putting women friends first. But when it came to knitting sweaters, I remained low on Crystie's list.

She insisted she hadn't made that many sweaters for men, that most were for herself. Fine. Was that better? Was I supposed to be comforted by the knowledge that she wouldn't put my needs before hers even once in thirty years? I had no equivalent tangible proof of devotion to offer her, as my craft skills are next to none. But what about the times I sat with her while she ate ice cream, me just smoking a cigarette because they were calorie-free? What about sticking by her during the Quaalude years? What about the countless hours I spent listening to her boyfriend problems? Didn't all that qualify me for a hand-knit sweater?

Our friendship was not without its bumpy times. Sometimes I thought Crystie's reluctance to knit for me was a form of punishment. She felt I was bossy, and she worked hard to break away from my judgmental influence in her early twenties. We survived that. We grew to have differing values about money and politics. We survived those, too. Old resentments caused Crystie to sometimes make humorous, cutting remarks about me in front of friends. I suffered them for years before a heart-to-heart talk in our forty-first year washed them away and made our friendship stronger than ever. We lived on opposite coasts, took different paths through our thirties, and yet continued to be each other's most trusted confidante. Still, no sweater.

We saw each other through the untimely deaths of our mothers and through the realization at age forty that we might be single women forever. We nursed each other by phone through broken hearts and rejoiced together when Crystie found true love at forty-three, and suddenly, miraculously, I had a significant love interest to bring to her wedding. We were both married for the first time within ten months of each other, to men who were also marrying for the first time. We joked about the irony of her, the Jewish princess, ending up with a labor organizer while I, the radical, got a nice Jewish doctor, but our lives seemed weirdly, wonderfully parallel. Then we tried to have children. At our age, it would take every miracle of modern science and we both used them all. That's when our paths diverged again. I was blessed with twins, and Crystie did not conceive.

The strain on our friendship was the most wrenching ever. I could not confide all the minutiae of my new life as a mother without hurting her; she could only pretend to revel in my happiness. Marriage had already cut our phone conversations back by hours each week. Parenthood widened the gulf between us. We confided less and less in one another. I didn't dream of hounding her for a sweater now.

☙☙☙☙

Then, when my girls were three, a mutual friend invited Crystie and me to her fiftieth birthday in our hometown, St. Louis. This was a great opportunity for us to meet in the middle and hang out together, without husbands or children. It was like old times. We loved it; we loved each other. We touched on the strain of the past few years, but mostly just delighted in each other's company, talking long into the night. We were moved by how nourishing it felt to be together and rededicated ourselves to maintaining our relationship.

The next November would be my fiftieth birthday. Crystie came for a visit early that summer. She bonded with the twins and we talked more openly than ever about the pain of the fruitless adoption process she and her husband (mostly she) were still pursuing. Before she left, she asked me to accompany her to a knit shop and pick out a pattern for a sweater.

Over the next few months she reported on the sweater's progress: It was a different color than I had chosen but she thought it would suit me. She had to rip it out and start

Robyn and her twin girls.

over because she had made a huge mistake I didn't fully comprehend. She was developing some kind of carpal tunnel syndrome and had to take long breaks from knitting, much as she hated to. She suffered two more close calls with babies that were nearly in her arms before they were snatched away. Despite her assurances, I didn't expect her to finish the sweater. I felt guilty for still wanting it, but I did.

It arrived the following November, just over one year late. I lifted it from the package and held it close for several moments before I even tried it on. It was the most elegant sweater I had ever owned. Its radiant blue stood out like a jewel in my closet of blacks and muted grays. And I could feel the love each time I put it on.

Wearing Crystie's gift, at long last.

One month later, Crystie got her miracle baby girl. Finally we could share the ecstasy and terror of being older mothers. We began to fit in more phone calls, comparing notes on everything from infant sleep habits to vaccinations to waning libido. She understood at last how hours could slip away watching a baby grow.

Crystie chuckles at the luck that made her finish my long-awaited sweater just before she became too busy with the responsibilities of motherhood. I like to point out to her that it might well have been that knitting project, with all the letting go of envy and selfless love it entailed, which led to her getting the baby in the first place. At the very least, there's a certain satisfying synchronicity there. We both are grateful for the fortune or fate that brought us our daughters. And my wish for all three of them is a future filled with life's treasures, like enduring female friendships and exquisite hand-knit sweaters.

≈*Robyn Samuels*

the best-laid plans: on (not) knitting

🐏 I never thought about learning to knit before I had a baby. Two months after my son was born, though, inspired by the lovely blanket his godmother knitted for his baptism, I clumsily picked up some needles and a "learn to knit" book and tentatively cast on. At that time, I was reveling in my new maternal status, and I imagined rosy domestic scenes of myself knitting cuddly, adorable sweaters and hats while my baby cooed peacefully at my feet. Yeah, right. More often than not, I worked on knitting projects furtively, frantically completing a row or two before my son woke up from his too-brief naps. Somehow, though, I managed to snatch time for enough stitches to complete a few small projects, and I soon felt brave enough to tackle my first sweater.

A baby sweater would be perfect, I thought—challenging enough to give me a sense of accomplishment, but not so big as to seem overwhelming. I leafed through pattern books at leisure, planning to sew a sweater for my son to wear the next winter. That's when we got the phone call. It turned out that my husband's sister Erin, who had just gotten married a few months before, was now expecting a baby. Pregnancy test in hand, she was calling everyone she knew, eager to share her excitement.

Now, I'm not a superstitious person. I regularly spill salt, step on cracks, and walk under ladders without even thinking twice. But when it comes to pregnancy, I'm a worrywart. When I was expecting my son, we waited more than three months before telling anyone, even our parents. I bought his crib and stroller before his birth, but only under duress from relatives. Even my baby shower seemed somehow to be tempting fate. So to me, Erin, who was spreading the happy news even before her first obstetrician appointment, seemed downright foolhardy. When I discussed Erin's pregnancy that night with my much more optimistic husband, he glanced at my open knitting book and suggested that it would be "really great" for me to knit a sweater for Erin's baby.

In theory, this was an idea I could get behind. Wouldn't it be nobler to make my first sweater as a gift rather than selfishly keeping it for my own baby? Wouldn't it be thoughtful to present Erin with a one-of-a-kind, handmade gift rather than yet another coordinated outfit from BabyGap or copy of *Goodnight Moon*? But in reality, I was nervous. What if something happened during pregnancy or birth? Here I would sit, left with a one-of-a-kind, handmade reminder of an incredibly sad event. My husband dismissed my fears, pointing to my own easy pregnancy and robust baby as evidence that all my worries about pregnancy were unfounded.

Cheered somewhat by his confidence, I tentatively turned my attention to this new project. I set aside my patterns in eighteen-month sizes, intended for my own rapidly growing boy, and I hesitantly examined patterns in smaller sizes, suitable for a baby who would be less than four months old when autumn leaves began to fall. Not knowing whether Erin's baby would be a boy or a girl, I looked for unisex patterns and for neutral colors, making careful notes as I considered whether each pattern would be suitable for a novice knitter like myself.

Meanwhile, we received regular progress reports on Erin's pregnancy, both from Erin herself and from my husband's parents, who lived much closer to her than we did. It was a tough pregnancy right from the start. Erin was plagued by morning sickness. She was unable to keep down any nutritious food and lost close to twenty pounds. Completely exhausted for the entire first trimester, she began missing work. Her acne, which had disappeared when she was in high school, resurfaced with a vengeance. In short, if she hadn't been so thrilled about being pregnant, she would have been miserable all the time. I, worrywart that I am, mentioned to my husband that maybe Erin's difficult pregnancy was a sign that I should wait to make the sweater. My husband reminded me about an article we had both read that contended that worse morning sickness equals a healthier baby.

Then we got another phone call from Erin. "Guess what!" she said. "We had our first ultrasound, and it's a boy!" Even as we both congratulated her, I found my mind drifting back to those sweater patterns. Now I could make that sporty boys' pullover, or maybe that cute cardigan in a blue and white stripe . . .

My reverie was interrupted by Erin's voice on the other end of the line. ". . . And it's another boy, too!" That's right—it was twins. Surely this explained Erin's incredible morning sickness, her recurrent dreams about having two babies, her early need to move into maternity clothes even though she hadn't gained any weight. As I expressed my surprise and joy to Erin over the phone, I felt a sinking sensation in my stomach that I couldn't quite explain. Then, after we hung up, it hit me. My first big project, my first sweater, was actually going to have to be two.

Now that we knew the sex of Erin's babies, there was no reason why I couldn't get started, and if I wanted to finish the sweaters before the babies started kindergarten, I needed to get into gear. I went to the local yarn store and bought enough yarn for two blue-and-white striped cardigans in a six-month size, made sure I had the right supplies, and double-checked the pattern, but I was unable to convince myself to start the project. The yarn, overflowing my knitting basket, seemed to reproach me every time I walked through the living room or picked up the much safer knitting project I was working on, a scarf for my mother. I couldn't figure out why I was unable to start knitting those sweaters. Was it that I was scared to start such a big project? Was I, with my woefully unpredictable gauge, worried about trying to make two sweaters the exact same size? Or was it that deep down I was fearful about these unborn babies?

All my fears seemed to be confirmed when we got a tearful phone call from Erin a couple of weeks later. Because of her high-risk pregnancy, her doctor had ordered weekly detailed ultrasounds, and the first one had revealed a disturbing disparity in the twins' weights. The doctors were concerned about something called twin-to-twin transference syndrome (TTTS), a rare but serious phenomenon that could threaten the lives of one or both twins.

Erin's doctor was clearly preparing her for the worst possible outcome. As soon as I hung up after our scary conversation, I packed the soft blue and white yarns out of sight. Now was the time for praying, not for knitting.

The next several months were tense, as we received weekly phone updates on the twins' weight from Erin and her husband or from my in-laws. Each day I prayed that those tiny boys would grow stronger, that the weight of the smaller twin would catch up with his larger brother's. Mostly, though, I felt sorry for Erin, whose pregnancy would be remembered as a period of stress and fear rather than a time of hopeful anticipation. She couldn't allow herself to look forward to the babies' birth with joy. Instead, she could only wait, helpless, for each week's ultrasound and a new estimate of the babies' weights. Like Erin, I too was paralyzed, unable to pick up my knitting needles, even when my husband suggested that knitting the sweaters might be a good outlet for my nervous energy, a more productive use of my hands than biting my nails to the quick.

Week by week, ultrasound by ultrasound, ounce by ounce, the babies' weight differences slowly equalized, and the prognosis from the doctors seemed less dire. As Erin reached the twenty-fourth week of pregnancy, the time at which premature babies actually stand a chance of survival, I quietly got my yarn back out of storage. As I wound my first yarn balls, my hands were shaking so much that I dropped the balls even more than usual. As my own baby, chortling and clapping, practiced his new crawling skills by retrieving my dropped yarn, I took his glee as a good omen for my knitting and for his tiny cousins.

Still, though, I wasn't able to start knitting, as I was sure that taking up my needles would spell certain disaster for the babies. Our whole family waited as Erin reached important milestones: the start of the third trimester, the point at which the babies' lungs were developed enough, and the week when she could give birth in her local hospital rather than travel more than 100 miles away to a facility with a more sophisticated neonatal intensive care unit. The doctors continued to monitor the babies' weight closely, and soon they expressed a new concern; although the boys' weight difference had evened out somewhat, their overall weight gain was not progressing on schedule. As soon as the babies' lungs matured a little more, the doctors said, it would be healthier for them to be outside the womb than to risk further growth retardation by continuing the pregnancy. As Erin's doctor appointments increased to four or five per week, my husband and I waited each day for news that the babies had been born.

Finally the phone call came. That morning, Erin had gone in for her scheduled appointment. After the customary ultrasound, the doctor told Erin's husband to go home and get Erin's hospital bag. They would perform a C-section that afternoon. As we waited for the news, I drove my husband crazy, cleaning the house frantically, remaking all the beds, finally just pacing through the kitchen after I ran out of projects. Thoroughly frustrated with me, he sat me down, handed me my yarn, and told me to knit. Finally, I did, and it felt remarkably good. I started my gauge swatch at the time of Erin's

Needle Notes

Does that itchy sweater bother you? To soften it up and reduce itch, wash the sweater with soap (not detergent) and rinse thoroughly; repeat one or two times. Then give the sweater a cream rinse with your favorite hair-conditioning product. Block dry and see if it doesn't feel softer than before. If the itchiness is still a problem, try wearing a silk undershirt between skin and sweater.

scheduled C-section, and finished it just as the phone call came that evening. It was from Erin herself, tired but ecstatic. The boys were small, but strong. Parker and Garrett were going to be just fine.

That night, I started the first sweater. Late into the evening, I knit and imagined Erin gingerly holding those tiny babies. I knit slowly at first, then faster as my hope for the babies and my confidence in myself grew. The next day, Erin's husband e-mailed us pictures of Parker and Garrett. In one of the pictures, the babies seemed ridiculously tiny, their heads the size of the orange that had been placed in the bassinet for comparison. Over the next weeks, I pictured those tiny heads, covered in hospital-issue stocking caps, as I knit my nephews' sweaters. Suddenly I knit with a vengeance, eagerly shaping their sweaters after months of depriving myself of the chance to knit them. Even as it seemed impossible that the babies would ever grow enough to fit into their six-month-size cardigans, I imagined myself knitting my hopes and prayers for their health into each blue or white stripe.

Knitting a sweater is a lot like having a baby. You can dream about how it will end up, you can think you've planned for every eventuality, but sooner or later, you realize that even the best-laid plans can sometimes go awry. A pattern with garbled instructions, a sleeve that's too long or too short, a delivery that's difficult, a baby with a hidden health problem—these are the chances we take when we create something from nothing. In the end, though, what matters is the process itself, one that will never bear fruit unless we conquer our fears, pick up our needles, and give birth to our creations.

Norah Piehl

PREEMIE AND NEWBORN EYELET CAP
BY BARBARA SELESNICK FOR STITCHES FROM THE HEART

GAUGE:
6 sts = 1 inch
8 rows = 1 inch

SIZES (HEAD CIRCUMFERENCE)
Preemie Small: 10" (27–31 weeks)
Preemie Med: 10.6" (31–34 weeks)
Preemie Large: 11.3" (34–36+ weeks)
Newborn Size: 13"

MATERIALS:
Sport Yarn
#3 and #5 dp needles
1-inch-wide satin ribbon

INSTRUCTIONS:
Cast on 56 (60, 60, 64) #3 needles
K1, P1 rib for 4 (4, 6, 6) rows.
Change to #5 needles and knit 1 row, increasing evenly to 60 (64, 68, 72).

EYELET ROW: K1, K2 tog, YO
Knit on these (60, 64, 68, 72) sts. until 2½" (3⅛", 3½", 4½") from beginning.

SIZES 1 & 3 ONLY: Knit next row decreasing 4 stitches evenly. <u>56</u>, (64, <u>64</u>, 72)

© 2002, Barbara Selesnick.

SHAPE TOP:

Size 4 only starts with: *K7, k2tog* (64 sts), then knit next row.
Sizes 1 & 3 only start with: *K6, k2 tog* (56 sts), then knit next row.
Size 2 only starts with Row 1 below.

Continue in pattern established below:

Row 1: * K5, k2 tog* (48 sts)
Row 2 and all WS rows: Knit
Row 3: *K4, k2 tog* (40 sts)
Row 5: *K3, k2 tog* (32 sts)
Row 7: *K2, k2 tog* (24 sts.)
Row 9: *K1, k2 tog* (16 sts)
Row 11: *K2 tog (8 sts)

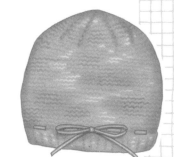

Weave yarn through remaining sts and pull tightly. Weave in ends.
Weave ribbon through eyelet row, tying a bow in center front.

*For information on joining Stitches from the Heart, a nonprofit
organization, contact:*

Kathy Silverton
12021 Wilshire Boulevard #507
Los Angeles, CA 90025
Toll-free (866) 472-6903
E-mail: *StitchesFromHeart@aol.com*
Web site: *www.StitchesFromTheHeart.org*

knitting and the farm invasions

꩜ "My name is Denise and I am an alcoholic . . ."

The group leader opened the meeting. Her dark ensemble accentuated her sunken eyes. Her parchment skin had been in the South African highveld sun too long. In the smoke-filled hospital lounge, drab curtains hung listlessly and great pitchers of orange juice dribbled on the table. Shabby chairs, with gashes in the upholstery used for hiding prohibited substances, muttered obscenities. Denise leaned over to the next person in the ring with a meaningful gesture, and a benevolent, gap-toothed grin.

"My name is Lara and I'm from Zimbabwe," said the patient who shared my ward. She brought her knitting to the meeting. Balls of wool danced, the colors of the Zimbabwean flag—emerald, gold, ruby, onyx, white. Lara said little; she looked pained and winced often. I watched her stabbing stitches with her thin blue hands.

When Denise testified, it became evident why she looked like a

bag lady. "I was fabulously wealthy . . . once." She spoke
like a society matron with crisp and pedantic enunciation.
"I was accustomed to high society . . ." I gaped at the coral
lipstick leaking into the ancient cracks around her mouth.

I didn't look too hot myself, admittedly, in tired pajamas
that needed a wash. I had lost the fresh pair brought in by my mother-
in-law when she brought my baby to visit me. I wasn't going to a fashion
show though, so what the heck, I'd decided to go for the sandwiches.
Like every other weary being in that room, the sandwiches also seemed
to know the depths of misery—weeping lettuce, dribbling tomato tears.
Only Lara's knitting danced. I watched the loops weave into colored
blocks as the pattern steadily emerged in the lengthened piece.

As I stared at Denise I felt confident that my lipstick didn't
clash with my socks, but when I looked at my socks, I was ashamed.
They were not a pair, so I sat on my feet.

The assembled gathering listened in stony silence to Denise's
tales of outrageous parties, fine food, better wine, and of the who's
who of the Sandton set, dripping with diamonds and gushing Gucci
as they fell *dronklap* into the swimming pool. Then the sandwiches
took over and I lost the plot.

"Being an alcoholic sounds glamorous," whispered a bologna
sandwich. "Perhaps, in a backward sort of way . . ." mused the
chicken mayonnaise. "That woman talks too much!" said cucumber-
and-parsley. Tick-tick-tick went Lara's needles.

I wanted to tell them—the sandwiches—to be quiet, but I knew
they would give me lip straight back. Instead, I said, "Hi, I'm Liesl
and I have postpartum depression. I came to monitor the sandwiches . . ." All the patients smiled nicely, because they're used to
people talking crap in the Hospital meeting.

Denise asked me to read a passage from The Good Book, or The Big Bang, or some such. This reminded me of Sunday School, where I was always the best reader. I read; this helped the sandwiches lie still. Everyone listened, eyes closed.

Lara looked at me and smiled. The jewels of her knitting melted suddenly and flowed back through her hands, into her bones. Her face colored a little redder, her eyes a bit bluer, and she winked.

When I had finished, the sandwiches' lament started up, at which point the unoccupied chairs began a slow circling around the room. One particularly shabby-looking one hovered over the platter and shook its head. It waggled its scratched legs from side to side. "On no accounts must the sandwiches be consumed," cautioned the chair.

Lara, folded up her knitting and took me by the hand. As we headed out, the duty sister spotted us.

"What are you doing in the rehab meeting, Mrs. Stacey?" she asked, handing me my lost pajamas.

"Wanting sandwiches . . ."

"What were your pajamas doing in the pot plants?"

"Dunno . . ."

"You are not supposed to go to rehab meetings."

"Oh." I stared at her blankly.

"You know you are not in rehab, don't you?" she said, testing my reality perception.

"Yes."

"Why are you here, then?"

"Because I'm possessed by the demon Leviathan?" I said, testing her sense of humor.

"No!" She didn't think it funny. "Because the Psychiatric ward is full."

"Aha!" She failed the test, but I thought better of pointing it out.

"Come along, dear," she ordered. "You can have sandwiches from the nurse's station."

⚮⚮⚮

A few days later, the chairs had settled and the sandwiches had quit their nonsense. The medication I had been prescribed was starting to work and I was beginning to feel vaguely normal for the first time in six months. I chatted to Lara, admiring the ethnic geometry of the Fair Isle pattern she was knitting.

"Who is the lucky recipient of this beautiful sweater?" I asked.

"Little Joe, my youngest."

Lara brought out a small photo album and showed me a photo of the baby. "The barefoot one is Kate—she's six—and that's Thandi, our maid." Thandi beamed, holding the baby. Red earth and scrubby thorn trees filled the background. The baby did not smile.

"How old is Joe?"

"Just a year."

"Hey, my Keith is a year too, actually fourteen months yesterday."

"Who looks after him while you're in the bin?"

"My mum-in-law; he adores his Granny."

"Yes, I saw her arrive at visiting time."

"God, it must have been hard for you though—to leave your baby."

Like me, Lara didn't seem to belong to the unit. She didn't have the glazed look of the alcoholics that were drying out. She seemed extremely normal in every sense of the word—except for her grey pallor and blue fingers.

"You're from Zim?" I asked.

"Yes, Marondera, near Harare."

"Amazing! What do you do there? Farm?" I have never been to Zimbabwe.

"We live on a farm, but I'm a doctor. There's a manager that works the land because my husband is a professional hunter. He takes rich Americans into the bush to shoot lions. He is often away."

"Why are you really here? You're not a druggie."

Lara laughed.

"I'm dependent on pethadine, actually."

"How so?"

"I got hooked because I prescribed it myself, for pain management. I have a serious heart condition . . . and I need surgery. The cardiologist insisted I get off the stuff before the operation. The anaesthetic risk is high and it's made worse by my addiction."

∽∾∾∾∾

A letter from Lara arrived a short while after we were both discharged from the hospital, inviting me to visit her with my children. It was full of happy news of her health, the baby Joe and Thandi. I was glad to hear from her and delighted at the invitation. I desperately wanted to see Zimbabwe, as the country was rumored to possess an aching and exquisite natural beauty. I didn't feel able to make the fourteen-hour drive alone, as African border posts are not for the faint of heart. My year-old son was teething and my four-year-old daughter had recently developed asthma. My husband was unable to take leave.

A darker letter arrived the following year. According to Johannesburg newspapers, things in Zimbabwe were not going well. Lara's handwriting looked like broken sticks.

The surgery seems to have been quite successful, and—good news—I am really pethadine-free. The Americans still come hunting and aren't scared of a couple of rowdy war vets making a rumble in the jungle. Unfortunately, it means Joseph is away often. I miss him of course, but real dollars pay real bills . . .

My practice is quiet, though. A lot of people have left the area. The upside of that is that I like having time with the kids. I'm knitting an Aran sweater in an off-white pure cotton thread right at the moment.

I am afraid sometimes, the political agenda is changing. Our staff are skittish, seemingly terrified of every shadow. A number have left suddenly, for no apparent reason. Little Joe cries for Thandi, who was the real queen of his heart, anyway!

Shortly thereafter, the Zimbabwean farm invasions began. Headlines were grim: "War Vets Slaughter Farmers."

I wrote back to Lara, offering her a place to stay if her family needed to flee. The letter was returned. The post office stamp obliterating her name read: UNKNOWN AT THIS ADDRESS.

♋♋♋

I took my children to the park today. On the way there, I saw today's headline on a poster. It was another chilling reminder of the chaos and bloodshed up north.

"Zimbabwe on a Knife Edge!"

While my children scrambled up the slide, jostling each other to reach the top first, I watched a young black woman minding a tiny boy. She called his name and he grinned at her. Then he raced off in the opposite direction. She jumped up off the picnic blanket and chased her toddling charge up to the swings. "Kgali's coming to push you!" she called aloud.

The baby squealed with delight as his nanny caught and tickled him, and placed him on the swing. Soon she swept him off and covered his squealing protest in kisses. "Let's get some juice now, Josh," she said as she coaxed him back to the rug covering the dried grass. First, she handed him a bottle of orange juice, then she pulled a sweater for him out of the carryall on the back of his pram. The late afternoon wind had risen.

It was a hand-knitted Fair Isle in bold colors, similar in style to the one I had seen Lara knitting eight years earlier. I covered my face and wept.

—*Liesl Jobson*

"Babies are necessary to grown-ups. A new baby is like the beginning of all things—wonder, hope, a dream of possibilities. In a world that is cutting down its trees to build highways, losing its earth to concrete . . . babies are almost the only remaining link with nature, with the natural world of living things from which we spring."

—EDA LE SHAN

bootie call

a tale of pregnancy, longing, and really bad nausea

ॐ I discovered I was pregnant on a Monday. There I was, fresh from a weekend knitting workshop, spreading gorgeous skeins of workshop yarn around my living room, just to get a better look at them. This was truly lovely yarn. Colorful, magical, luscious. Yarn you'd like to get to know better. Yarn you want to spend time with. Yarn so soft you'd take it to bed with you if your husband didn't already think this knitting thing was getting out of hand. And then I felt dizzy. Sit-down-so-you-don't-fall-down dizzy.

Could it be? I had wanted a baby for years, but we'd only recently "removed the goalie," as my husband described our cessation of birth control. Later that day, a drugstore test confirmed it. We were pregnant! Break out the double-pointed needles! Booties must be knit!

Later that week I returned to the skeins in my living room, only to find that something terrible had happened in my absence. The yarn had changed, transmogrified, become deformed. The colors were muddy, the texture scratchy. Worst of all, it smelled. Oh, how it smelled! Like a neglected barn. Like wet athletic shoes. Like a plate of German potato salad abandoned at an Independence Day picnic, only to be rediscovered in record heat on the 6th of July. This yarn was disgusting, revolting, nauseating. To look at it made me dizzy. To touch it was to tempt Vesuvius. And yet, here it was, scattered all over my living room, no one to remove it but me.

I accomplished the feat on my hands and knees, discovering I could hold off the retching if I took deep yoga breaths and kept my head tilted at a 45-degree angle. I wish I'd have thought to wear gloves or use tongs to avoid touching the foul stuff, but my wits were not about me. Instead, I crawled from one skein to the next, carefully pinching its belly band, then—using the dirty-diaper method favored by sitcom dads—turning my head and dropping it into a plastic storage bag.

My revulsion was not confined solely to the workshop yarn. Over the next few days I discovered that all yarn made me queasy. A glance at my once-beloved pottery urn of needles caused my throat to tighten and my jaw to clench. Pattern books, magazines, and fliers for knitting retreats brought on such dizziness I would be forced to a horizontal position, lying flat on my cool kitchen floor. There on the linoleum, I had plenty of time to think, and so I worried for my unborn child. Dozens of friends' babies had come home from the hospital in my hand-knits. Now my own daughter would be naked, exposed to the elements.

Needle Notes

Remember the practicalities of dressing a baby when you choose a pattern. Is there a row of tiny buttons that look great but will be a huge hassle on a squirming infant? See if you can find a pattern that's easier to maneuver on a real-life baby.

Or worse, consigned to a department-store hair shirt, a cloying bunny hot-glued to her chest.

More often, I admit, I thought about my pitiful self. I had imagined that during my pregnancy a bunch of earthy neighborhood women would somehow appear at my side to teach me lullabies and coo over the tiny sweaters that flew from my needles. Weeks, months into my pregnancy and the earth mothers had yet to arrive. Fine. I was beginning to recognize them for the lousy stand-ins they were, anyway. I was lost in L.A., far from my Michigan roots, and alone. (Okay, I had a devoted husband and lots of friends, but like daydreams, self-pity is not bound by logic.) I wanted my mother. And her mother. And all the women of my family. I felt disconnected and abandoned.

This was not a completely new feeling for me. Once, ten years before, I had felt equally lonely and in desperate need to connect with my family. It was then that I first learned to knit.

♋♋♋♋

As a child, I was proud of my mother's needlework skill and would enter a room twirling my skirt, shouting *my mom made this*! A school uniform put off the inevitable through junior high, but by high school I wanted designer jeans and store-bought sweaters. I wanted Calvin Klein and the Gap; labels I saw as the passport to popularity. Homemade clothes fit better, but store-bought clothes fit in.

Likewise, I disdained the homeyness my mother's handiwork symbolized. The version of feminism that trickled down to the early '80s high-school set had nothing to do with honoring women's work and everything to do with women in the workplace. I planned to get my degree, move to Chicago, and live in a skyscraper. My apartment would be white, my furniture chrome. I would eat out every night and never stitch so much as a blouse button. I stayed true to this misguided sense of a woman's roar through college, until love and graduate school brought me to L.A., where my classmates were as icy and sharp-edged as I thought I wanted to be. Instantly, I was homesick.

To admit an appreciation for my mother required maturity still beyond me. I decided to miss my mother's mother, instead. A Québecois immigrant who spoke French in her sleep, Grandma LeBlanc performed loaves-and-fishes miracles, unraveling a single potholder and knitting it into a family's-worth of mittens. In addition to knitting, she could sew, tat, crochet, embroider, and quilt; she often clothed her family by remaking the discards from the wealthy homes she cleaned. Over sweet, milky tea, she would tell me stories of her own grandmother, whose huge floorloom dominated their farmhouse, or about the winter she spent knitting a yellow dress that fit so well she blushed and never once wore it in public. My grandmother had passed away while I was in L.A., and I longed for the twin hummings of her battered Singer and the French folk songs she sang under her breath. And so, I bought a book and taught myself to knit, my yarn a woolen umbilicus that connected me to her and through her to home.

Soon I was knitting all the time: mittens and Christmas stockings, a lace shawl for a friend's wedding, and a too-heavy Aran for my huntsman brother. I knit baby sweaters as gifts for lucky friends and family. At least I did until the day I took the baby test myself, found it blue and myself green at the thought of knitting a single stitch.

∽∾∽∾

The knitting nausea lasted ten long months. And then, one November morning—shortly after my husband took a photo of me at full girth—the first undeniable contraction. I searched out a notebook and jotted down the time: 9:25. On the opposite page were notes scribbled during the knitting of a chartreuse carriage coat, another baby gift. I looked over the notes . . . not a hint of nausea. On my desk sat my pottery jug full of needles. I picked up a set of Susan Bates circulars and felt . . . fine. A pattern book of simple baby clothes presented itself, then several balls of steel-blue, washable cashmerino. I took a deep breath and knit a swatch.

9:50: *another contraction.* I did gauge-math. Miraculously on target, I braved the cast-on.

10:30: *contraction.* An inch of stockinette appeared on my needles.

Noon, and the contractions were ten minutes apart. Eight yarn-overs made eyelet openings through which a pink ribbon would pass. I divided stitches front and back.

Twelve contractions later I called my husband. "Come home," I said casting off the neckline. Contractions five minutes apart, I finished the ribbing on a delicate cap sleeve. I had been humming "Alouette" for more than an hour.

∽∾∽∾

It would make a better story if I finished knitting my new daughter's dress as we pulled into the hospital parking lot—or while in the throes of labor. Honestly, I don't know when I finished the dress.

I thought that I had left it unfinished, in pieces, the final sleeve never even cast on, but I found the dress not long ago; knit, finished, and blocked, a pink ribbon weaving in and out of eyelet. Perhaps I finished it half-consciously, during one of those sleep-deprived early days I can hardly remember. Or maybe my mother, who came to stay with us during my first heartbreaking week back at work, found it in my knitting basket and made it whole. I've yet to ask her, because I'd rather persist in the belief that my grandmother had something to do with it, humming as she worked, knitting another miracle.

Linda Urban

Four: Ode to the Humble Sock

"Isn't it awful that cold feet make for a cold imagination and that a pair of woolen socks induce good thoughts!"

—FRANZ GRILLPARZER

Think of fire-engine-red toenails, shocking in their vibrancy, yet hidden, secreted away in daily working pumps or inside sweaty tennis shoes. At the end of the day, the shoe is peeled away in a tantalizing striptease, revealing the real you—you of the ruby toenails. The edgy woman with scarlet dreams finally peeks out.

Or, better yet, think of exotic silk underthings with fine lace trim—not the scratchy lace that's an irritation, but soft, stunningly intricate, handmade lace. Picture the most beautiful bras, panties, slips, and camisoles you can imagine, the kind you want to touch and appreciate. Now imagine wearing these extraordinary undergarments for a regular run-of-the-mill day.

Going to work with them under your corporate suits, or wearing them under your mommy wardrobe of jeans and T-shirts. Only you know that there's more to you than meets the eye.

Hand-knit socks, for me, are the same kind of mysterious luxury, speaking to deep layers of extravagance, yet casually hidden away, as if the opulence I possess need not be shown off. In fact, the luxury can only be fully appreciated as long as the secret remains. Only my feet know the real me.

Think cashmere socks, the softness pillowing your feet, wrapping them like a perfectly fitting glove. Or argyle, with the complexity that boggles a mind all gathered together just to honor your tootsies. Even plain socks, hiking socks, daily wear socks: When hand-knit, they're a treasure, a comfort unseen, uncommented upon—and the more rich for their silent nature. They hint at the depths of the full, manifold you.

Knitting socks, for yourself or others, is an uncommon gesture, speaking to layers of intimacy. The process itself can be a wild adventure. The first time that you make the ribbing—having to make sure that you don't twist your work where the two sides of the cast-on stitches come together to make that seamless tunnel of sock—seems difficult, hard to manage. You knit on in perfect faith that when the time comes to make gussets or turn the heel, you'll have what it takes. And when you do turn that heel, you stop to marvel at what you've done. You hold the work in your hands with sheer amazement: it worked! "I turned this heel," you stop to proclaim to whomever might be nearby. "Check it out: it's a sock!"

Once the first two or three socks slide off your needles, it becomes easy. You can make a pair a week and offer that special comfort to all the people you know. Socks don't take the kind of

Herculean effort and determination required of making larger projects, like sweaters or afghans. With socks, you can knit for all the people you've wanted to.

The humble sock. The mundane sock. The lavish sock. Hidden away. Your secret and mine. Make a sock for yourself or someone you love, feel the richness on your feet when ensconced in so much love, and then go about your day, all the while knowing what cradles your instep. You'll never look at socks in the same way again.

"If you want a golden rule that will fit everything, this is it: Have nothing in your houses that you do not know to be useful or believe to be beautiful."

—WILLIAM MORRIS

traveling socks

It's time to change my life, time to shift its patterns so I go less often into buildings and more frequently out into the weather, so I cast forty-eight stitches onto a long knitting needle and begin to make a sock. I count twice. Then as I work the first row I divide the stitches evenly among four short needles that are pointed at both ends. At the end of the row, I join the stitches into a circle. One sock at a time.

I start to knit around, working a tube in a simple ribbed pattern that will stretch as the sock slides onto my foot and then contract to fit snugly and warmly around my ankle. A well-fitted sock surrounds the foot like a second skin, secure throughout. A good sock doesn't fall down, and these will be good socks. By knitting plain, everyday socks, I have learned how many stitches to use with this particular wool yarn and these size-2 needles to make socks that fit me well. These will not be elegant socks. They will be sturdy, foot-cushioning, hiking socks.

In a plain canvas bag that allows my knitting to go with me everywhere, I have placed yarns of many colors, each transformed from the perfectly usable, loosely formed, machine-wound factory package into an egg-shaped, hand-rolled ball of medium density. In the process of winding these balls—a meditative preparation for the tasks of design and construction—I have already touched each strand of every color along its entire length. These yarns have already known the temperature of my body, and I have already known the warmth of the fibers.

In the bag I have placed a deep brick rose, a light water blue, and a green reminiscent of the way that spring's buds appear like an aura around the still-skeletal branches of willows emerging from winter. There's also the indigo blue of ages past and cultures far away, the creamy sand color of dunes. A few of these colors I don't like by themselves. Yet if I only include my favorites, the socks will be bland.

My fingers pass the stitches from needle to needle, growing the fabric one stitch at a time. I know that these socks will not be ordinary, but I don't know what they will be like. As the ribbing of the sock's leg lengthens under my fingers, I pull new colors from my bag and begin to work in subtly colored stripes.

While my choices of colors and their placement make an obvious contribution to the work, some aspects of my craftsmanship operate on a level that only serious knitters would notice. I alter the ribbing pattern on the color-change rows, in order to keep the lines between the colors straight and clear despite the ribbed texture. Over the years, I have learned to do this without thinking. I vary my stripes in width and color, inventing a pattern that pleases me.

At the end of the ribbing for the leg, I do two things. Because the remainder of the sock needs to be less elastic than the leg, I change to a smooth pattern of stitches called stockinette. I also begin to knit, instead of stripes, the elements of a map.

The ankle area consists of twelve rounds of stitches. This is slightly more than average length for an ankle area, but I have learned what works for my body. In this part of the sock, my map begins to trace rolling terrain, footpaths, a mountain spring. Reddish earth, the dusty green of sage in summer, a few specks of June-yellow wildflowers in a meadow.

I reach the heel, where I will work back and forth on my needles to form a cuplike shape that will cradle the back of my foot with each step. I slightly alter some of the stitch forms as I work them, slipping the tip of my needle in from the back instead of the front of the stitch or sliding a loop back and forth quickly between the needles, shifting its angle in the process. Almost no one will notice how the stitches mirror each other on the sides of the heel. Here I knit the shape of a tarn, a high mountain lake, its deep, cool waters filled by the spring on the map of my ankle.

When the lake's gently undulating waves lap the shore of my instep, I begin to work around the tube again, creating a sheath for my arch. Roads appear on the map, first gravel, then paved. I knit trees and parks. Because these socks don't map buildings or traffic, the parts of my life that I want to leave behind, this is as tame as the landscape becomes. Each time I change colors, I invisibly secure the ends of the yarn so the fabric remains completely smooth.

Needle Notes

When you want to knit socks that will have a nice pattern, investigate yarns that are dyed specifically to create patterned socks. For example, Fortissima Colori by Schoeller Stahl (available at your local yarn store, or try *www.patternworks.com*) is a self-striping sock yarn that allows you to create a Fair Isle look without the work. It's an easy way to make an impressive sock.

As I reach the toe, I start to knit foothills. Stony, irregular paths will rise in front of my feet when I wear these socks, and the forms on the fabric need to be ready to join them. I knit a few prairie-dog burrows, then a hawk circling in a clear sky with pale, translucent clouds on the horizon. No rain today, although the weather can change quickly. The world of my socks changes from map to layered horizons. It prepares to move through space and time.

I have learned the capacities of my handcrafted wool socks by wearing them in deserts, in rainforests, in alpine tundra. They expand and contract as needed. When damp, they still keep me warm. I trust my hands. I trust the socks they are forming.

Continuing to work my spiral path around the tube with needles and yarn, I knit stitches together in a specific sequence to shape the toe, decreasing the fabric so it will close and encompass the end of my foot. There will be no seam, and no lumps to interfere with the comfort of my walking. I knit together the final few stitches and I invisibly secure the last end of yarn.

When I make the second sock, I use its partner as a reference, but not a restrictive one. Although they will become a pair, these socks will not be identical. My right and left feet experience the world from slightly different perspectives.

When I have finished both socks, I put them on my hands for a moment. I splay my fingers to extend the fabric so I can inspect the patterning and the workmanship, and I hold them in front of my eyes, turning them so I can see all the angles. While this lets me examine my work reasonably well, hands are only makeshift inhabitants for socks.

I put the socks on my feet, lace my well-worn hiking boots over them, call the dog, and walk out the front door.

Nobody knows where I'm headed, not even me. No one else knows, or cares, what I'm wearing inside my boots. But I do.

Deborah Robson

WANDERING SOCKS
BY DEBORAH ROBSON

This sock style is my favorite for everyday wear
with jeans or hiking pants, and with boots or Birks.
I made this pair with leftover yarn from a sweater—at worsted weight, they worked up quickly, even at the close gauge I chose
to increase their durability. I added interest (for both knitting and
wearing) with texture rather than color. Knitting at its best is very
personal and idiosyncratic. So is this pattern. It's a workmanlike
design, not fancy but not boring.

Thanks to Priscilla Gibson-Roberts for my favorite heel- and toe-
shaping method and to Barbara G. Walker for the pattern inspiration.

SIZE: Woman's extra-large—foot 10 ⁵⁄₈ inches long, and fairly narrow.
For advice on adjusting for other sizes, see Priscilla Gibson-Roberts'
Simple Socks Plain and Fancy (Cedaredge and Fort Collins, Colorado:
Nomad Press, 2001) or Ann Budd's *The Knitter's Handy Book of Pat-
terns* (Loveland, Colorado: Interweave Press, 2002).

MATERIALS: Worsted-weight, about 4 ounces.

GAUGE: I'm hard on socks. I crank the gauge tight for durability, and
I use this tight gauge throughout the foot. Although worsteds usually
do well at 5 stitches/inch, I worked this pattern at 7½ stitches/inch,
measured on the smaller needles that I used for all but the upper portion of the leg ribbing.

NEEDLES: Check your own needle/gauge combination. Many people will
use sizes 3.5mm (US 4) for the majority of the sock ("smaller needles")
and 3.75mm (US 5) for the upper portion of the leg ribbing ("larger

needles"). I work loosely and achieved this gauge on sizes 2.5mm (US 1) and 3mm (US 2–3). When it's time to work the heel or the toe, life will be a whole lot easier if you use a set of five double-points (rather than four) or the two-circular-needle method Cat Bordi teaches in *Socks Soar on Two Circular Needles: A Manual of Elegant Knitting Techniques and Patterns* (Passing Paws, Washington: Passing Paws Press, 2001).

RIB PATTERN: Barbara G. Walker's "Lace Rib," from *A Treasury of Knitting Patterns* (Pittsville, Wisconsin: Schoolhouse Press, 1998; page 48), adapted for circular knitting and charted.

ABBREVIATIONS:

k	knit
k2tog, k3tog	knit 2 (or 3) together (right-leaning decrease)
p	purl
SSK	slip 2 stitches individually knitwise, then knit the 2 stitches together through their back loops (left-leaning decrease)
SSP or SSSP	slip 2 (or 3) stitches individually knitwise, return the 2 (or 3) stitches to the left needle, and purl them together through their back loops
yo	yarn-over
knit-side yo	yarn forward under the needle, then over the top to the back (this is a normal yarn-over)
purl-side yo	bring yarn to the back under the needle, then over to the top

LEG: Using an elastic cast-on and the larger needles, form 65 stitches and join for circular knitting. Work three rows of p2, k3 ribbing.

Then begin the "Lace Rib" pattern:

Row 1: *p2, k1, yo, SSK,* repeat around.

Rows 2 & 4: *p2, k3,* repeat around.

Row 3: *p2, k2tog, yo, k1,* repeat around.

Repeat these four rows for 2" (5 cm). Change to the smaller needles (which will be used for the remainder of the sock) and continue the pattern for a total of 6" (15 cm) from the cast-on edge. End with row 2 or row 4 (plain rib).

ANKLE: In stockinette, work 13 rounds even, decreasing 1 stitch in the first round (64 stitches). If you are working with five double-points, make sure there are 16 stitches on each of the four holding needles; if you are working on two circulars, have 32 stitches on each.

HEEL: Work the heel on 32 stitches (with five double-points, two needles' worth; for two circulars, one needle's worth).
Shape back of heel:

Row 1 (knit-side facing): k31 (leaving 1 stitch unworked at the end of the needle); turn.

Row 2 (purl-side facing): purl-side yo, p30 (leaving 1 stitch unworked at the end of the needle); turn.

Row 3: knit-side yo, k29; turn.

Row 4: purl-side yo, p28; turn.

Repeat the pattern established in rows 3 and 4, working 1 stitch less in each row until 14 stitches remain between the yarn-overs, ending with the purl-side row that is worked purl-side yo, k14; turn. (Throughout the back of the heel, work an odd number of stitches in the knit-side rows and an even number of stitches in the purl-side rows before turning.)

Shape base of heel:

Row 1: knit-side yo, k14, correct the mount of the yo loop on the left needle (slip it as to purl, then slide the stitch back to the left needle; the leading side of its loop will be on the front of the needle); knit together the yo and the next stitch; turn.

Row 2: purl-side yo, p15, SSP the yo and the next stitch; turn.

Row 3: knit-side yo, k16, correct 2 yo mounts individually (as in row 1), k3tog (2 yos and the next stitch); turn.

Row 4: purl-side yo, p17, SSSP (2 yos and next stitch); turn.

Repeat the pattern established in rows 3 and 4, working 1 more stitch in each successive row, until all stitches have been worked, ending with a wrong-side row (purl-side yo, p31, SSSP); turn. (Throughout the base of the heel, work an even number of stitches in the knit-side rows and an odd number of stitches in the purl-side rows before turning.)

Next row: knit-side yo, k32, correct mount of final yo loop by slipping it purlwise: 34 stitches on the needle(s). Slip the final yo to the next needle and k2tog (yo and first stitch on next needle), k30, SSK (last stitch of round and yo)—64 stitches remain on all needles.

FOOT: Return to working around all 64 stitches and knit even in stockinette until the foot measures 8½" from the back edge of the heel.

TOE: On the 32 stitches of the upper half of the foot, shape the top of the toe the same way as the back of the heel, then the bottom of the toe the same way as the base of the heel. There will be 34 stitches in this "half" of the sock: 32 regular stitches and a yo at each end.

With kitchener stitch, join the toe stitches to the 32 stitches that were resting, treating the yo at each end and its adjacent stitch as one. Secure the final tail of the yarn. ●

k2, yo, p2

My first encounter with knitting was in my last year of elementary school in the 1930s. We girls were introduced to spool knitting, and at recess we whipped out our spools to get in a few inches before the bell rang. Forget chasing boys. Friends provided us with odd lengths of yarn, which we traded. I have no recollection of making anything creative with my very long knitted tube.

Then came the real thing: learning to knit the adult way. I used Pick Up sticks for needles and kept a goodly supply at hand, because breakage occurred regularly. When I was working on my first job, I used to take my knitting with me on coffee breaks. On one occasion, after hearing a call in my direction, I turned to see a red-faced young man frantically rolling the yarn onto the ball I'd inadvertently dropped. I trust those long-ago boyfriends enjoyed their hand-knit socks, with a mending sample enclosed.

During World War II, my mother and her best friend took up knitting, but only for the armed forces—nothing frivolous or family-oriented. I can remember returning home from work, and the two friends cheering because each had dropped stitches and needed me to set them straight.

They took their projects everywhere, even to civic music concerts. Once, a certain well-known opera star spoke from the stage. "Please turn up the house lights so that our knitters won't drop their stitches." There may have been other knitters in the audience as well.

Whenever I'd bring a date home, the poor young man became an instant model for my mother's finished knitwork. When the war ended, my mother returned to crocheting a bedspread for my brother and his wife, a work that had been delayed by her war-effort knitting.

Even my husband-to-be, Hinkle, knit. (We've been married for fifty-six years now.) Beginning in World War II, before I met him, he worked in upstate New York during a colder-than-usual blustery winter. Staying indoors at night held more allure than did venturing out. He and the other members of his engineering group learned to knit from a local young woman.

Some years later, he and I were driving from North Carolina to California on our honeymoon. I decided to knit socks for my groom as a useful way to while away the hours. At intervals, I'd hold up sock number one for him to see. "A little longer would be nice," was his repeated comment. When I finally called a halt to these socks,

The family that knits together . . .

made of a beautiful blue wool, they extended over his knees!

After we had settled in California, we had a silly idea. We took a photograph of the two of us in our nightclothes, sitting up in bed, knitting. It's a color slide, taken on a whim. Many years later, our children reproduced the photo onto T-shirts for our wedding anniversary. Faded by now, the shirts are still in our dresser drawers.

Once, when my husband was recuperating from a long siege of influenza, he decided to make argyle socks for himself. I would be his teacher this time, with the television going, of course. So that our friends would believe that he'd actually made them, using bobbins and all, he knitted his initials into one sock. He worked laboriously on this project. As soon as he recovered enough to return to work, he abandoned his knitting needles, but he still has the socks as proof.

A few years ago, I was actively involved in church activities. I always took a knitting project with me for extended meetings. One of the older men in the group frequently asked about my knitting. Finally, he told me that he'd been taught to knit in elementary school during World War I. He was so pleased with the results that he, in turn, had taught his mother to knit, a reversal of the usual roles.

Libbie Greer

"Choose your friends by their character and your socks by their color. Choosing your socks by their character makes no sense, and choosing your friends by their color is unthinkable."

—ANONYMOUS

out of chaos:
a knitter's journey

🐚 My descent into illness was sudden. Between one day and the next, I lost everything that I believed defined who I was: a rewarding job, sports, travel, active social life, and my photographic memory. I woke that morning feeling fragile, perhaps coming down with flu. As the day wore on, it was a struggle to carry out my duties at work; by quitting time, I was barely able to walk the short distance to the bus stop. That night I ended up in an emergency room, enduring a multitude of tests and leaving without any concrete answers. I suffered through fevers, infections, labored breathing, deadweight fatigue, and severe vertigo. I was certain that I was dying and that no one would know why. It would take another two months before I received a diagnosis of Chronic Fatigue Syndrome, also known as CFS. No cure and no treatment, I was told, except rest.

Being housebound and confined to bed for months led to a feeling of isolation that was demoralizing. I left my bed only to take care of the most basic bodily functions. The simple act of showering took me hours to recover from, and washing my hair turned into the equivalent of an endurance sport. My social life became nonexistent overnight. Reading was almost impossible because my eyesight was blurry and unfocused and I could not concentrate or remember what I had read. Instead, I listened to stories and music on CDs that a friend created for me. Phone calls were an immense drain on my limited energy. I could listen to others talking but it was a struggle to reply, and I often nodded off while I was still clutching the phone.

It was inevitable that I would lose some friendships along the way, especially those that relied on daily contact to sustain them. It was unnerving to realize that the glue that bonded many of my work relationships was gossip and social chatter. I didn't have the energy or desire to participate anymore. Gradually, the phone calls and e-mails died away, and, in the ensuing silence, I was left with the knowledge that those who had stood by me through this struggle were the friends I had always been able to count on in the past. Family members accepted that I was ill, but they were confused and unsettled. I had always been the healthy one, and my family had a difficult time coming to terms with my inability to recover quickly.

The emotional pain of giving up my work, sports, and social life was devastating. I had been employed as a records coordinator with the same company for twenty-five years. While it was hectic and demanding, I loved the work and the constant testing of my memory skills and research abilities. Now, I couldn't remember the names of simple everyday items. I would write myself reminders on sticky notes and then wonder what they meant and who they were for. I had always been a physical person, and my husband and I were ardent cyclists and kayakers. We traveled the Oregon and California coasts many times over the years, and just the week before we had completed a 100-mile cycling trip in Washington State. Now, it was an effort to walk up our stairs; rarely did I complete the climb without at least one stop to recover my breath and slow my racing heart.

Living for three years with a chronic illness that is extremely debilitating in terms of energy and concentration has been difficult, and I have grieved for the loss of lightness and energy that had been with me since childhood. The one creative activity that I refused to let go of during this crazy time was my knitting. Even when I felt so sick I couldn't get out of bed for days at a stretch, I kept my knitting in a kit beside my bed and would work a few stitches at a time, stopping when I felt too weak or dizzy. When it was just too much of an effort to pick up my needles, I would visualize my next design, planning the most delicious colors and softest texture to whet

my knitterly appetite. At 4:00 A.M., when sleep eluded me, I fantasized about creations concocted of luscious mohair and creamy cashmere, in shades of purply plum and brilliant turquoise. During this period most of my knitting projects were small—hats, scarves, bookmarks—as I found myself overwhelmed by larger items and the volume of stitches needed.

I was at a very vulnerable stage in my illness—depressed, unable to move from bed most days, and coping with a constant feeling of nausea and vertigo—when I decided that I would learn how to knit a sock. In retrospect, I can't believe that I subjected myself to this seemingly hopeless task at the same time that I was suffering from a severe inability to concentrate for more than a few minutes at a time. I'm not sure why I was determined to learn this process, but I remember thinking I had to do this one thing in order to feel better about my situation. It was important to me that I learn something new. It felt like everything had been taken from me: my wired energy, quick wit, ability to reason, verbal skills, and manual dexterity. Somehow I had to regain a sense of pride in learning a new skill and producing a finished item. My mom had tried to teach me sock knitting years earlier, and we had ended up weeping with laughter, our hands intertwined in the yarn and needles as she tried to guide me through the steps. Now, I was on my own, but I could hear my mother's voice inside my head, telling me that it was easy once you got the first few rounds completed.

How can any sane human hold four small pointy sticks with two hands and somehow manipulate a ball of yarn with a fifth stick and expect to produce a wearable garment? And what's all this garbage about gussets and heelflaps and other strange expressions, I would mutter to myself. I would feel the frustration boiling inside me as my patience wore down and my fingers fumbled over and over again with the needles. Who invented this barbaric method of torture, and whose idea was it that I should learn this stupid parlor trick? My hands became slippery with sweat as I concentrated, biting my tongue in the process. Oh wait, I just moved over to the second needle without dropping or twisting any stitches. When I managed to complete several rounds without stabbing myself or having a stroke, I could have wept with sheer exhaustion and pride. Now I couldn't stop no matter how tired or ill I felt. I pushed myself to complete the top ten rows of ribbing, and then I lay back in bed, a huge grin spreading across my face as I contemplated the beginnings of my first sock.

When I had become fairly competent at producing a wearable sock, I showed a friend how the process evolved, while the sock was still in the gusset-decrease stage and spread over four needles. He was in awe, turning the half-finished sock over and studying the design. I suddenly realized that I had just created something extraordinary, and that I had gained a skill that few people attain. For weeks I kept waiting for someone to bestow a special commendation on me for my impressive needlework, and I would bore friends and relatives with minute details of my sock in progress. Finally, when the initial novelty had worn off, I was able to take this new proficiency in stride. (I could hear my friends sighing with relief.)

Through many traumatic moments of this illness, I would pick up my knitting and escape inward, weaving the pieces of my broken life back together with the knit and purl stitches. When I was scheduled for a series of medical tests, I took my latest sock project along in my carryall and knitted my fears and anxieties into the pattern. This was one pair of socks I could never part with. Months later, when my condition had stabilized and I had acquired some stamina, I was able to knit a vest for myself using all the blue shades from my yarn stash, changing colors midstream as I ran out of yarn or my interest waned. It turned out to be a size too small and the final result did not match my expectations, but it felt satisfying to complete something unique.

Recovery has been slow with many relapses. Some of my symptoms have improved, while others have remained the same or worsened. The friendships that endured through this upheaval have become even stronger, and the new friends I've encountered along the way—most of them dedicated knitters like myself—have added vibrancy to my life. I had been married to my best friend for thirty years when this illness struck, and, while we have encountered many emotional and physical adjustments in our relationship, we have survived and grown even closer.

Knitting has given me a link to the life that I inhabited before I became ill; because of it, I've managed to retain a fragile sense of self and feel creative in the process. Every project that I've completed during these past three years has given me more pleasure and joy than anything I created before. I'm also fussier about details and mistakes now. If this is all that I can bring into being at this moment, then it's going to be the very best. I've ripped out more projects than I've completed, but the effort has been worth the final results. I find that when I'm immersed in my knitting, I'm able to forget all the emotional and physical upheaval in my life and just concentrate on knitting one beautiful stitch at a time. Nietzsche's observation that "out of chaos comes a dancing star" is an accurate portrayal of the process of trying to find creative and spiritual expression in the midst of suffering. Knitting has helped me to accomplish that objective.

Mary Anne Mitchell

Five: In Sickness and in Health

"And as for sickness: would we not almost be tempted to ask whether we can in any way do without it? . . . I doubt whether such pain 'improves'—but I do know it deepens us."

—FRIEDRICH NIETZSCHE

Illness is part of the human experience, and so naturally it is a common thread in the knitting community. When I set out to research my previous book, *Zen and the Art of Knitting*, however, I had no intention of delving into the world of physical ailments, even though my own story of learning to knit involved a torn Achilles tendon and the inability to walk. Surely others learned to knit and took comfort from knitting for other reasons, I'd figured. Yet as I researched the book, two intertwined themes kept emerging: that knitting for someone who is ill is a healing act, and that knitting when you yourself are sick helps stave off the blues that can accompany illness. Knitting speaks to the desire to heal, to see happier days, to rejoin the human race with vigor and wholeness, to be a contributing member of society.

When the *Zen* book was released, I was asked to read at local bookstores. I planned to bring countless balls of yarn and armloads of knitting needles to the readings. I'd teach everyone to knit and then read to them as they worked. But what about all the little scraps of knitting we'd produce? I didn't want those to be wasted.

At the time, I learned that a friend of a friend, Ellen Chavez Kelley, a wonderful author of children's books and a respected poet, was about to undergo a bone marrow transplant. She had been battling non-Hodgkin's lymphoma and chronic lymphocytic leukemia for a few years and wasn't making much headway. This transplant offered her the best last hope. That's what we'd do with the squares! I asked everyone at the readings to think of Ellen as they knit and told them that their squares would be fitted into a healing shawl that would accompany Ellen as she was taken to the doors of death with the transplant and brought back to life again.

After the first reading, a woman approached me with tears in her eyes. She carried a large bag filled with a nearly completed afghan. She pulled the beautiful, richly textured work from the bag and held it out to me.

"I've been knitting this," she told me, "for

Needle Notes

Knitting a prayer shawl for someone who's ill need not be difficult. I created one by asking everyone who wanted to participate to knit up a three-inch square in garter stitch, thinking of the sick person as they knit. When I gathered the squares, I was worried that they wouldn't fit together. But by placing them on the living room floor and moving them, the finished shape showed itself. Every square had its place and the odd-looking pink square, which wasn't quite square at all, ended up as a heart in the center. The main thing is to get all the people who are concerned about the ill friend involved. It's the love and intentions that count.

someone who's sick. Until tonight, I didn't know who that someone was." She paused. "It's for Ellen."

She explained that her sister had died the previous year from breast cancer. She'd knit valiantly throughout her sister's illness, but was now bereft of someone to knit for. She'd continued to knit her healing wishes into this afghan, confident that when the afghan was ready, the person who needed it would appear. And here she was.

She sent the afghan to Ellen, who later told me, "You know, it arrived the very day I checked into the hospital for the transplant. It was there exactly when I needed it!"

At the readings, we completed the healing shawl, made up of little squares of our hopes and prayers for Ellen. She returned from the lengthy ordeal tired and worn out, but with new hope. As of today, Ellen is cancer-free. The first selection in this chapter is the poem she wrote in response to that anonymously offered gift.

the shawl

I enter the hospital, that kingdom of machines,
plastic and steel. The same day a package arrives—
a shawl in a tissue paper bed, sent as leaves fall,
burning swath of Pecos autumn.

Knit for me by a kind stranger
the shawl gazes back, weeping,
patient, glorified, its colors steeping me
in protection.

Two days later, as frozen cells infuse,
I seep slowly out, disintegrate, fade.
Days trickle by. I hold the shawl close,
wrapped in its swallows and nests.
It curls against me through long nights,
delicate as a cat's tongue, my familiar,
my whisper, my silken beast.

Midnights, so cold, as if dipped in death—
violent chills beat me breathless.
I am starved for wind, roses, rain. In the shawl
lie morsels of a living earth, some part of me
not lost after all.

A month later I leave the hospital,
shuffle through November's dark sea,
seeking the door. Even those who love us best
cannot stay the loneliness of such a walk.
Still the shawl flames, beacon in bleak silence,
candling a memory of home. Part feral,
part goddess, it is constant as stone and fire.

Weeks pass. My son drapes bright prayer flags
over the door. I step through, shaky-kneed,
breathing hard beneath my mask. Thin-skinned,
fragile, my senses sharp and clean as ice,
I look up to snow healing the mountains, to clouds
shepherding orange groves and palms, a flock
of bright green parrots on red flowered branches.
This is not the world I left three months ago.
This is a new place, to be entered slowly.

In Bushman society, women control
the men's dance. Women are life,
give and care for life, are the source.
I wear the shawl in remembrance of transformation,
of each gesture and pattern formed from the hands
of woman into the hands of woman.

I stand in the place
where two lines cross
and go on.

🕊Ellen Chavez Kelley

quiet please—knitting zone
(or, the boys at their knitting)

"QUIET PLEASE—KNITTING ZONE." This is the sign on the doors leading to the ward where future pilots, Canadian and British lads about nineteen years of age, are recovering from training accidents. Some are severely burned; others have fractures. Those whose hands have been damaged sit in their hospital beds wearing large white plaster of Paris casts on their arms while struggling with the garter stitch.

It's 1942, and I am among the medical personnel at a fifty-five-bed operating unit of a Royal Canadian Air Force (RCAF) hospital on a flying training station located in endless corn and wheat fields some 20 miles southwest of Hamilton, Ontario, Canada. I am in charge of the Orderly Room, where I work for five doctors, transcribing and typing all case histories and monitoring all admissions and discharges.

One additional duty has been added. I am an adept knitter, so I teach those boys with damaged hands what to do with a ball of wool and a pair of knitting needles as part of their prescribed physical therapy.

"I'm putting this needle right between your thumb and fore-finger," I tell a knitter almost before his cast is dry. "Use your fingers like pincers. That's it!"

For the boys, the knitting is a way to keep their muscles from atrophying. As for me, I love to knit; I begged to be taught it when I was a child of four growing up in New-foundland. But these boys have their sights set on becoming heroes in the European skies. Right now they feel like "knit wits," so they are dealing with this recuperation time by razzing each other and anyone else on the base:

"I hear Teddy Jones has got the tire."

"Again?"

"Third time, I think. Been taking it everywhere except bed."

Helen (waving) and her sister, before the war.

Not surprising. Teddy Jones is a slight English lad full of the old Nick (that is, always ready for mischief). He views life as a place to have fun, break a rule or two, and stretch the limits.

The RCAF does not let such behavior go unnoticed. Any young aircraftsman caught in some flight indiscretion—for Teddy it is invariably low flying—receives the Tire Punishment. For one week the perpetrator must roll a tire along with him wherever he goes.

"Maybe he's falling in love with his Goodyear," Thomas, a red-headed soldier, jokes.

"We'll knit him a scarf and he can keep her treads warm!"

Discipline is serious business on the station. A rule abused brings a consequence served. My own transgression is to knit in bed after the 9 P.M. curfew. I'm caught, and I'm grounded two Saturday nights in a row.

Many of the boys are far more adventurous than that.

There is a custom on the base that invites everyone to have an Initiation Flight with a pilot and a co-pilot. I've heard the boys at their knitting talking about these times. The flight is supposed to be smooth, with no jerks. But the cut-ups like Teddy Jones—or anyone keen on a girl—will navigate the flight quite differently. They "stall turn," a tactic guaranteed to scare the bejesus out of many a young nurse.

"She couldn't take it," I'd overhear from a knitter the next day. "Went for the tube."

The only place to throw up on these planes is the same tube designed for pilots to relieve themselves. No girl wants to use that!

Helen with her husband, Ted (who is _not_ Teddy).

My Initiation Flight arrives on a beautiful, clear Saturday in the spring. Sid Reynolds and Joe Lawrence take me up. I see the winks between them right after takeoff, but I am counting on my athletic sturdiness and the fact that I'm a girl with a habit of winning track meets. I have guts and a strong stomach to boot.

Joe stall turns once, then again. Over a farmhouse we lean so far left that I can nearly reach down and pick a sunflower. I need to swallow a bit of something that's come up from my tummy, but I'm not telling. If I just keep my eyes on the horizon I'll be fine. Blue sky; cornfield: watch the line in between and take slow, deep breaths.

We're heading back. I can see the long, low buildings and the Parade Square where we must pass inspection each morning with our buttons polished and our shoes shined. I'm focusing my mind on such details when Joe accelerates, banks, and flips her over. For ten horrific seconds I'm flying upside down, my helmet chinstrap flapping into my eyes, the breath all but sucked out of me.

I will not be letting the boys at their knitting tell of my using the tube. I will tough it out. Green, but still holding my breakfast down, I thank the boys for their unforgettable ride, exit the plane, and walk gingerly toward the nearby baseball field and the closest bench. A game of hardball is being played, but I am not watching. I am saying prayers of thanksgiving. I am waiting for my world to stop twirling and my ears to stop humming. But I am definitely not watching the game.

It comes as a great surprise, then, when I wake up in our hospital, smelling the familiar freshly starched sheets, the clinking of beakers.

"For goodness sakes, Helen," says the group captain and my track coach. "Why didn't you duck? That ball came straight at you."

"If you felt as woozy as I did, you'd find being knocked unconscious preferable too."

Not long after I'm back on duty, Teddy Jones comes in. His crash had been serious. He overshot his landing and barreled into an aircraft hangar. Teddy was lucky to have survived an accident so costly for both himself and the Canadian government!

For weeks he barely speaks, but then the old glint returns in his blue eyes and he's ready to fight boredom any way he can. I get him going on the knit and the purl, but he's forever dropping a stitch.

"I've got a dent in my rows," he calls out.

"That's because you've let a stitch slip, Teddy. See, you did it four rows back."

"Can you fix it, Helen?"

I never tell Teddy or the others that to a skilled knitter, a dropped stitch is a serious no-no. Avoiding it in their twelve stitches on the needle and for indeterminate knitting lengths of four and five feet becomes a worthy challenge. The boys work hard, assuming this must be for some noble cause, perhaps to help someone stave off a storm or even save a life.

We don't say otherwise. We don't say the noble purpose is to rehabilitate their hands so they can feed themselves, tie their shoes, blow kisses to loved ones for the rest of their lives.

Our cheery Teddy Jones stays so long in the ward that we ask him to deliver the mail in his wheelchair. Rascal that he is, he acts the buffoon, mixing up the letters so that Ben gets Larry's letter from his sister and Lew reads a love note from someone else's girl.

But all is always forgiven with Teddy. And when he leaves to go back to England, he turns sentimental and becomes one of only three patients who ever asked for this particular farewell gift.

"Please," he asks us, "would you give me a ball of wool and a pair of needles? I'm a knitter, you know."

And so we do.

≈Helen Wright Davis,
in collaboration with Judi Davis Healey

"The human spirit will endure sickness; but a broken spirit—who can bear?"
—PROVERBS 18:14

tea cosy

It was an English knitting pattern, as she couldn't follow the American ones.

For standard teapot, use three 50 gram balls.

She chose yellow wool. Not that she cared for yellow particularly. It was simply the color closest to her when they brought the box around.

"Which color would you like, Mrs. Paddison?" the nurses' aide had asked, her milky round face leaning above her. Too many freckles to be attractive, probably, but pleasant enough. No use saying "It doesn't matter" to one like her. Of course it mattered to her. Everything mattered to her. She was very young and very earnest.

So Brigid Paddison chose the yellow. One, two, three balls, according to her pattern. It was a buttery yellow. The wool was smoother than she was expecting. A particularly expensive brand, she noted, that was donated to places such as this.

Loose knitters—one pair each: Nos. 7 and 9. *

They would be English needles, the smaller numbers being the largest needles. The American needles were all the other way. Brigid was an English knitter, and she couldn't be sure with the American system, even after all this time. She couldn't be sure if she was a loose knitter anymore, either. Everything she did was tightly screwed down, held taut and rigid against the crushing pressure that was suddenly her life. Even her lips, she realized, were pursed and drawn as she scanned the pattern. The pattern was in a book that the nursing-home aide had put on the arm of the chair earlier, open to this page.

She put down the wool, aware suddenly that she had been holding it close all this while. She didn't put it far—just moved it from her arms, where it was clutched to her chest, down to her lap. It looked stupidly bright on her gray skirt.

Average knitters—one pair each: Nos. 6 and 8.

Perhaps.

Tight knitters—one pair each: Nos. 3 and 5.

No. Not tight, that was too much. She couldn't use number 3s. Just the thought of those thick number 3 knitting needles pushing off against one another like dead stiff fingers. She shuddered. Just too much.

Average she would be then.

Needles in instructions are for average knitters.

Just as well. Less thinking, all in all. She would use the 6 and 8 needles. Still a bit too big for her fancy, but she could manage. Didn't matter, really, did it? She had no interest in this; she was going to

*British needle sizes differ from American.

knit because the nurses' aide thrust balls of wool at her. Thrust a pattern book at her. She looked over at a small folding table to her right upon which her own needle case sat. (Tortoiseshell, inlaid, a gift—but from whom? She would have never bought such a thing for herself.) In there were her needles. She remembered the years they were hardly out of her hands, the years she knitted.

She knitted those years away, really: lost whole years to khaki scarves and khaki socks and khaki vests and khaki gloves. She kept her extra needles, invariably 9s and 10s (she had been such a loose knitter those days!) in that case. But when did she get that case? A Christmas present, surely. But she could not think of who would have given such a costly thing. Ah, well . . . not that it would change anything.

With number 6 needles . . .

Did she have number 6 needles in that case? No, she wouldn't have. She simply didn't have needles like that.

Oh, wait. Yes. She had forgotten. Besides the pattern book and the wool, the aide had given her a pair of each, numbers 6 and 8, British standard. Brigid must have told her she was an average knitter already. She didn't recall it, but there it was. The needles were tucked in beside her. The number 6s were blue plastic, not metal. Made in Canada.

. . . cast on 44 stitches.

How does one start again? A knot, then a loop . . . oh yes. Then there she was, casting on. The wool was lovely to pull through her fingers. Almost slick, but not greasy at all.

*First Row: K3 *P2, K2, rep from * to last stitch, K1.*

That was quite simple, especially with these large needles. She didn't like the plastic, though; it bent, even as she held softer and softer. And the blue against the yellow! Horrible. Somehow it made the whole thing, even with this expensive wool, feel thin and cheap.

She remembered the full blurry feel of the old boiled khaki wool. Secondhand wool it was, and it came from pulling apart old cardigans and vests, boiling the lot and rewinding and using it. Some lots were dyed. She forgot how they did it now. Was it onion skins and tea leaves? Or did they give her some packets to boil? Either way, it was hard, hot work. Sorting raveled wool into boiling pots of dye, and then lifting pounds of the sodden stuff out. You had to wring it out still hot, to string across chairbacks, or else it would dry and shrink into a waste.

Second Row: K1, *P2, K2, rep from * to last 3 stitches, P2, K1.
Third Row: as second row.
Fourth Row: as first row.

A little tricky—but not difficult. The "Double Moss" stitch, she thought back, that was what they called it. Made a nice change, really. All the knitting she had ever done was always garter stitch. "Fancy stitches use more. Garter is smarter: save wool!" they used to say. Both wars it was like that. Garter. The first time, the Great War, it was not so bad. Wool from Australia at first, before the unraveled stuff. Of course, thrifty housewives had always reused wool, but at the time, she was neither thrifty nor a housewife. Well, not at first. At first she was a girl. Later, after she married, she was a housewife. Then a mother. Then a widow. All in the space of two years. Such an awful lot of her life was completed in those two years, no time to be thrifty really. But, she was, in her own way. She had no choice about the wool. Australian wool went for Australian soldiers in the end; tired, overused English wool had to do for tired, overused English soldiers. Not that she cared. She knitted until 1918, but her own husband, her Will, he died the first day of the Somme, July 1, 1916. Young Will was born on the 25th, that same month. She had already had Ellen. Just nearly one year old, she was.

Work in pattern for approx. 5 inches, ending in a 4th row.

Ellen was a good child. Quiet, as older children often are. Will, now, Young Will, he was the opposite. Full of spirit. Never dull. Never still. Never quiet. Perhaps it was the lack of his father, or perhaps, Brigid thought, it was his father's high happy nature in him. Brigid remembered the two of them as two pairs of flashing gray eyes, two mouths that turned upward in easy smiles. They were both so young, they were, when they were killed.

She had only two photographs of her husband; they both looked like her son.

There, four rows done. Now repeat.

Repeat. Repeat. Her life was all repeat. After her Will died she thought there would be no more. Yet, there was Will, their son. And after that bloody war which she had knitted away, stitch by greasy stitch, she thought she would knit no more.

But she did. Repeated it all. Knitted from 1939 to 1945. Young Will was killed in action in 1941. She knitted after he was gone. Knitted with tired old wool from tired old vests. Khaki, always khaki, the loops endlessly repeating, becoming scarves, becoming socks. Her fingers growing tighter and tighter in their hold on the needles. She had had so many pairs of needles, then she had only a few. They were needed for the war. "Save Steel because Tanks and Aeroplanes require Metal" the saying went.

Still, she always managed, didn't she? Ellen left for America with some lad she met at a dance. Her new American family sent new American knitting needles.

There. Four more rows done now. She must try to loosen; even with these big needles her stitches were tight and close. Would take a great while to reach about 5 inches this way.

Of course, what else had she to do?

But, knitting? She had never thought about knitting after . . . after, when was that? Ellen's child went off somewhere, some war that no one needed to knit for. "No, Mum, they aren't cold, the heat is what bothers them over there," Ellen had written. Or, perhaps, rang up to say. She had had the phone on by then. She had her needles out, ready to knit, but they didn't need it. There was nothing she could do for that war, she was told. A bad war. She didn't knit. He came back, he did, her grandson.

Nearly 5 inches done. Took no time at all, did it? There. Time to look at the pattern.

With number 8 needles, repeat rows 1 to 4, 3 times.

Repeat. There it was again. Brigid looked at that ridiculous word. Repeat. The same thing over and over—granted, she could now put down these awful colored plastic needles.

Where were the others? Oh yes, she put them there, by her case. They were gray. Heavy steel. Marked "AERO," like all her needles were. Excepting those needles from America, but they were gone now anyhow. She could never feel right about those—the points were too sharp, the ends too heavy, the numbers all wrong—not like English ones at all. She'd left those behind, deliberately, when she'd been moved.

Ellen had moved her. Said it was too worrisome her being all alone. Worrisome! She'd been alone since Ellen left. Not that it was Ellen's fault. No, not Ellen's fault at all.

Ellen was a lovely child, and a lovelier woman. But, she had gone to America and Brigid didn't want to leave England. Ellen didn't insist. But she did impress upon her, over and over, how she, Brigid, ought really to move. How Brigid mattered to Ellen.

Continue on as follows . . .

So Brigid moved. Because it mattered to Ellen. Seemed so unimportant, in the end, to Brigid.

*Row 1: K2tog *K12, K2tog, rep from * three times.*
All even rows: K1, purl to last stitch, K1.
Row 3: K2tog, knit to last two stitches, K2tog.
*Row 5: K2tog, * K10, K2tog, rep from * three times.*
Row 7: K2tog, knit to last 2 stitches, K2tog.
*Row 9: K2tog, * K8, K2tog, rep from * three times.*

Sudden panic clutched. What if she missed something in the directions? They seemed fairly straightforward, but they were exacting. She must pay attention. Knit exactly so many stitches, knit two together at once, then exactly so many stitches again. And again. There was no way around it, she wasn't one of those for whom knitting was like breathing. She must, at times, concentrate. Shoulders and necks, turning heels, finger bits—how hard she had, at times, to work to keep her mind on them or else she would become lost. How long had she been working on these tricky rows now? Half a foot, then now this bit.

These needles were all wrong. More panic. And the wool, it was running out. How would she get more of this wool? Oh, yes. There were two more balls, just there. She'd tumbled them to the floor by her feet when she'd reached for the new needles.

She wondered where they'd gotten these needles. These steel needles. Now that Ellen had passed away and all. It was odd, wasn't it, to think that she, Brigid, was in a Home now. Paid for by Ellen's son. The one who came back from a war. He was so old-looking, had old children of his own. They wore their hair long. Much too long, really, but Brigid made no censure. They had names, surely, these people. What were they called?

Not good. Sometimes names wouldn't come. She felt her mouth purse up, her hands increase their grip. Life was all tight now, trying to make things that had raveled and slipped come back . . . as if, if only she could hold on long enough they would be able to be pulled back, and not lost to the depths completely.

How many rows now? She counted back . . . one, two, three, four, five of the decreasing ones. Add the even rows in with them, that was ten. Ten rows. Done so fast.

Row 11: K2tog, knit to last two stitches, K2tog.
*Row 13: * K2tog, rep from * to end.*

The yellow wool looked so bright on the duller gray of the number six needles. Knit, pull a bit on the wool, knit, pull, knit, pull . . . the gray flashed and the yellow flew between her fingers. A swirl of motion.

Cast off . . .

Knit, pull, knit, pull, pushing the loops off this time. Ending them as loops and making them an edge. There, she was done with it. The yellow thing was created. She couldn't make head nor tail of it. She put it down on her lap.

Knit another piece in same pattern.

Brigid carefully placed the gray needles next to her case on the table. Her tortoiseshell case, Will had bought it for her in France, on leave, in 1915. An anniversary gift.

She looked at the page in the pattern book on the chair arm. Where had she gotten this? No matter. It looked like a suitable pattern.

For standard teapot, use three 50 gram balls.

She hadn't three balls. There was one, and a partly used one. She would have to wait until the nurses' aide came. Unless, of course, she could unravel this thing here. Nice that it was yellow. She always loved yellow.

🪶Juleigh Howard-Hobson

"The web of our life is of a mingled yarn, good and ill together."

—WILLIAM SHAKESPEARE

Tea Cosy: "Hobson's Choice" Pattern
by Juleigh Howard-Hobson

For standard teapot, use three 50 gram balls (about 5 oz total)
Loose knitters—one pair each: Nos. 7 and 9. (US: 7 and 4)
Average knitters—one pair each: Nos. 6 and 8. (US: 8 and 6)
Tight knitters—one pair each: Nos. 3 and 5. (US: 10.5 and 9)

NOTE: Main instructions are for Average British Standard knitters.
Average US Standard directions given in parentheses: ( ).

With number 6 (US 8) needles, cast on 44 stitches.
Row 1: K3 *P2, K2, rep from * to last stitch, K1.
Row 2: K1, *P2, K2, rep from * to last 3 stitches, P2, K1.
Row 3: as second row.
Row 4: as first row.

Work in pattern for approx. 13 cm (5 inches), ending in a 4th row.
With number 8 (US 6) needles, repeat rows 1 to 4, 3 times.

Continue on as follows:
Row 1: K2tog *K12, K2tog, rep from * three times.
All even rows: K1, purl to last stitch, K1.
Row 3: K2tog, knit to last two stitches, K2tog.
Row 5: K2tog, * K10, K2tog, rep from * three times.
Row 7: K2tog, knit to last 2 stitches, K2tog.
Row 9: K2tog, * K8, K2tog, rep from * three times.
Row 11: K2tog, knit to last two stitches, K2tog.
Row 13: * K2tog, rep from * to end.

Cast off in purl.
Knit another piece in same pattern.

To make up, sew together knit sides facing out, leaving holes for spout and handle. If desired, with medium-sized crochet hook, chain stitch 5 cm (2 inch) length, attach to top as handle loop.

NOTE: This cosy was truly knitted by me, using British 7 and 9 needles (I'm a terribly loose knitter!) in 3-ply yarn. The pattern is based on an amalgamation of every tea cosy I ever knitted back in MacArthur Girls High School's Red Cross knitting club. And I knitted a lot of them. They say Australia leads the world in tea consumption, and I like to think I did my part. ●

Needle Notes

If your hands and wrists get achy or sore, by all means take a break. Do a few hand exercises to help: Extend your right arm with your hand flexed. With the left hand, pull back on the palm of your hand and your fingers to get a good stretch in the wrist. Switch hands and stretch some more, making sure to take the joints through their full range of motion. If the soreness persists, limit your knitting time to half-hour increments and avoid using large needles. If you knit English style—"throwing" your yarn—you might want to try Continental knitting to see if that will relieve the discomfort.

grammy and me

I sat on the footstool in front of Grammy and watched her nimble fingers move in a blur. The quick stitches jumped from one needle to the other, clicking as the sea-green sleeve grew longer before my eyes. Even at five years old I knew that Grammy was sure to finish the sweater in time for me to wear to Sunday morning church service.

I looked forward to walking with her to the Presbyterian Church each Sunday. Its grand dome lighted the vestibule with colored reflections of the sun, the colors falling like prism flashes across the hats and shawls of the ladies, touching each with rainbow hues. The gentlemen in their dark suits and black hats lingered outside greeting the members and visitors as they came up the steps, drawing the men aside. The men tipped their hats to Grammy and me as we passed their way and entered the warmth of the sanctuary.

That particular Sunday, March 14th, the weather was cold for this late in the season. The skies sparkled in a clear icy blue. A brisk breeze off the bay ruffled the palms and aralias surrounding the concrete building and swirled dust and leaves up the steep steps and around the Doric columns.

With the swell of the organ, the ushers opened the double doors and Grammy and I walked with the other ladies down the aisle to our usual pews. The men removed their hats as they entered the vestibule and slid into the seats their families held for them. I read the number for the first hymn, which was posted on a wood placard above the pulpit, and I flipped through the hymnal's pages to find it. Grammy looked down at the page and smiled, and then she turned a few more pages and lifted the book closer to her. She adjusted her reading glasses. I looked up at her as she said, "I know you know all the words by heart but I might need help if we sing more than the first two verses."

The minister rose, strode to the pulpit, and began to read from the scriptures. Playing with my church doll, I sat between Grammy and her friend Mrs. Jones. My doll's skirt was a lace handkerchief, and threads from its worn edges tickled my bare knees. One knee sported a Band-Aid, not unusual for a tomboy such as myself. Soon I leaned against my Grammy and dozed as the Reverend's voice rose and fell in a singsong cadence. As we stood for the benediction I felt a chill and pulled my sweater tighter around me.

We filed out of the warm church and Grammy chatted with the others as we waited to speak to the minister.

"Such a well-behaved little girl," a lady in a small black hat said to Grammy. The lady bent down and raised her veil to kiss me on the top of my head.

"Thank you, ma'am," I said, having learned to be polite even if I didn't like people kissing me in public.

Grammy reached down and smoothed my blonde hair. She took my hand in hers as we drew closer to the Reverend Samuels. "You're very warm. We should have taken off your sweater."

"No!" I said and stamped my foot.

Grammy raised her eyebrows but didn't say a word to me. In front of us a couple with an infant talked at length to the Reverend about the planned christening of their child on the coming Sunday. I leaned against Grammy. She put her hand on my forehead, and, without saying a word, she reached down and lifted me into her arms, stepped out of line, and hurried down the stairs. She almost ran carrying me home. The breeze felt chilly on my cheeks and I dozed, my head on her shoulder. I heard the click of her heels on the pavement and the swish of the screen door.

I must have fallen into a deep sleep, for when I opened my eyes I saw my bedroom. The curtains were drawn, darkening the room. My fingers picked at the bedclothes and I felt something cold against my body. The door opened. I saw the shadowy outline of a woman standing there with a bowl in her hands. She entered the room and placed it on a small table close to my bed. Another woman picked up a cool cloth from the bowl and laid it on my forehead. Then the two uncovered my legs and arms and applied more wet cloths.

I whispered, "I'm cold," but the ladies didn't seem to hear nor did they stop their ministrations. I drifted—sleeping, wakening, and sleeping again. Blurred sound and light roused me on occasions, but a sense of time eluded me.

"It's going to break soon. The shivering has stopped," a distant voice said.

"Thank God," another voice. It sounded closer.

Later that evening I awoke asking for Jell-O.

"Red or green?" I recognized my mother's voice. "I'll get both." She hurried from the room.

Grammy sat on the edge of my bed stroking my damp hair with her calloused hand. Momma returned and fed me small spoonfuls of red Jell-O, then green along with sips of flavored lukewarm tea.

∞∞∞

The next morning Dr. Newman came to check on my progress. He set his black bag on the bed and snapped open the latches. Reaching inside he brought his stethoscope out and unwound the rubber tubing. Next he took out his little rubber hammer and that thing he used to look in my eyes. After listening to my heart, checking my eyes, and thumping my knees, he led my Momma and Grammy into another room down the hall. He had left his bag and instruments on the bed. When the three of them came back into the room I had the stethoscope in my ears as I listened to my own heart.

"Well, well," Dr. Newman nodded with a smile. "Are you going to grow up to be a doctor?" Momma hurried to restore the items to the black bag.

"You should leave Dr. Newman's things alone," she scolded.

"Annie, don't worry. I'm just glad the child is doing so well. But don't forget what I told you. She will still need six months to recuperate."

I did not know what recuperate meant but I found out soon enough. It meant I had to be quiet and stay inside, and no friends could visit. Grammy spent hours sitting by my bed keeping me amused with games and puzzles. While I dozed she brought her knitting out of the fold-up tapestry bag and the needles clicked softly as they flew across the rows. I peeped from beneath partly closed eyelids and watched her. She dozed off sometimes sitting in the straight-backed rocker, and with the movement of her hands now quiet, I also drifted off to sleep. She continued to sit at my bedside entertaining me while she knitted doll clothes and a blanket for my doll's bed.

In mid-April a nurse friend of Momma's brought wrapped gifts, each numbered for every day until my birthday on June 9th. Number one was a composition book, which she had decorated with bright, colored paper flowers pasted on the cover. Grammy encouraged me to practice my letters in that book and soon I wrote stories about my toys, my Grammy, my Momma, and Wahoo, my big tiger-striped tomcat. With help from Grammy and Momma I invented companions and playmates that I badly missed. The Church ladies came often, loaded down with meals and dishes of fruit pies and cobblers, and

Joan and her Grammy.

my favorite, tapioca pudding. I even included them in my stories. Dating each half page like a diary, I diligently wrote every day.

Dr. Newman came to see me frequently and on the first of September declared I was well enough to go for walks on the lawn. Grammy and I strolled under the live oaks that made a leafy canopy across the front and side lawn. Every morning we watched as the yellow hibiscus opened their petals to reveal their ruby throats and turn the large bushes into a riot of blazing color.

"Can we have a tea party out here?" I asked, bored with my long confinement.

"Tomorrow we will do just that."

The next day Grammy arranged a table and three chairs in the shady side yard and placed the tea set on a white damask cloth with small matching napkins. Miss Winn from next door came around the corner of the house steadying herself on her cane. "Come take these cakes to the table before I drop them," she said.

I ran to her and retrieved the basket covered with a lowered napkin and walked beside her to the table. Lifting the corner of the covering I saw the tiny cakes and breathed in their delicious smell.

"The child looks much better. I see her color is coming back," Miss Winn said to my grandmother. "I understand it was rheumatic fever."

"Yes, Dr. Newman says there could be residual damage but he sees no sign of anything as of yet." Grammy patted my hand and settled in the chair across from our guest. "Would you like to bring your doll to the tea party?"

I raced toward the front door. "Don't run!" I heard Grammy's stern voice and slowed to a fast walk.

✺✺✺✺

One humid August evening, as I sat by a tall open window reading my favorite Nancy Drew book, I overheard voices from the next room.

"Come into the bedroom," Grammy said. "I want you to look at this." She led Momma into the room and I tiptoed behind.

The door stood ajar and I peered into the room from the shadows of the hall. Grammy turned almost facing the door but did not look in my direction. She unbuttoned her blouse and lifted her ponderous breast. In the fold against her rib cage, a red growth the size of my little finger's tip protruded like a thorn.

I stood staring through the opening, feeling guilty for spying and knowing I should leave. But I also felt hypnotized, unable to move, as I stared at the gross thing on Grammy's body. Backing away, I slipped down the stairs and out into the yard where I sat on the bench under the oak and pondered what I had seen. Tears stung my eyes and I knew something terrible was about to happen.

It took two years for her to die. At the end Mother sent me to a friend's house. The nurse who, so long ago, had brought me toys and trinkets to help me through my convalescence came to stay with Grammy those last few weeks. I was not there when she died.

Today when I remember her, I remove myself from the surgery that amputated her breast. The prosthesis she couldn't wear because of the discomfort and irritation. The pain she hid from her family. The swelling and weeping of fluid through the skin of her arm and her fingers, those nimble fingers, so puffy and swollen she could not bend them to turn a page or pick up a knitting needle.

Instead I remember the afternoons she rocked beside my bed. The tea party we had in the yard with my doll and the neighbor. I remember stories she told about a grandfather I never knew. Pictures she took during trips to the Rockies and the Smokies with my mother and her two stepbrothers when they were children.

Grammy was only sixty-nine when she died, not old by today's scale. I knew her for only thirteen of those sixty-nine years. But I remember watching the needles fly, and the sea-green sweater.

Joan Bond

hands

I love my hands. I have my father's hands. My mother's hands are thick and stub-fingered, two clumsy starfish. She has fat porcelain fingernails, which make it impossible for her to tie ribbons, unclasp earrings, or pick up coins. When I was a child, my mother couldn't button my dress or comb my hair without making worse knots or accidentally stabbing me in the face, and I've always been exasperated by her inability to be handy. I learned early to just steer clear of her hands. Better to do things myself. But I got my father's hands—long slender fingers, discreet tendons and veins, skillful and deft—and I've always felt a bit smug about that. My father is a sculptor, and as a child I loved to watch his hands shaping clay or carving wood, and I was awed by what he could do with them. I wanted to make things with my hands, like him. Biographies of the first Queen Elizabeth that I read as a child usually mentioned her elongated fingers and graceful hands, and so I liked to think of mine as regal, too. The hands of a princess, a queen. And descriptions often mentioned that Elizabeth was astonishingly good with a needle as well. She sewed her little prince of a brother his fine cambric shirts, and she learned to knit her own stockings with her exquisite, shapely hands. One biographer stated that "given the sheer length of Elizabeth's fingers, her control over them was amazing." Like my father, Elizabeth was an inspiration, and I learned to sew at an early age—as well as how to finger weave and needlepoint and macramé and embroider and crochet and knit. Grown-ups told me that with hands like mine I had the makings of a pianist or a surgeon. But I had no talent for music, no discipline for a decade of serious study. And, unlike my father, I couldn't sculpt—I had no skill with such raw elemental materials, and a lump of clay, despite any transformative effort, remained a lump of clay. I could turn a skein of straw into gold, though. I could happily focus for a stretch of hours on a sweater, an afghan, a scarf, winding balls of wool, snipping and weaving loose ends, counting stitches, admiring the growth of cloth from a mere scribble of string. Sculpting things from yarn. I really grew to love my hands because they were useful. Because they made things.

Knitting has always been the best. I like the steady-handed clutch on two needles, the click when they meet, the tidy vertebra of stitches sliding along the cool metallic spine. I like the elegance of cables, the elasticity of the loopy weave, the infinite variety of knit-and-purl design, the controlled dance of nubs and Vs. Knitting has always felt archetypal for me, ancestral. I can see cavewomen whipping up loincloths on whittled splinters of mammoth tusk, medieval nuns knitting themselves heavy gray stockings still sticky with lanolin, 1950s coeds working away on argyles for their frat-boy boyfriends. Knitting is both industrious and creative, practical and pretty, and when I knit I feel myself part of history.

Neither my grandmother nor my mother were knitters, but I like feeling descended from the line of Women At Their Craft, a generative force. And virtuous—no idle hands here. The iconic figures, Laura Ingalls Wilder and Madame Defarge, all knitting away for love or survival. I'm an obsessive knitter, at it in planes, trains, and automobiles, at the movies and in waiting rooms. I show up for appointments early, in order to get in a little knitting time. I'm the Girl Who Makes Things for presents at baby showers; to *oohs* and applause, I'm the Girl Who Is Good With Her Hands.

Writing has always felt akin to knitting. I used to write everything in longhand, and my penmanship, like my craftsmanship, was a source of pride. No wimpy, girly curlicues or flourishes for me—my handwriting was a clean and compressed expanse of tiny block letters, like a perfect stretch of stockinette stitch on size-two needles in fingering-weight yarn. At some point I dispensed with lower-case letters entirely, which lent each word, I felt, a certain conviction, lent each row a clear nap and definition. I wrote long letters to out-of-state friends, always stopping to admire the look of my words on my pages before folding them away in envelopes, exactly the way I stopped to admire the Aran stitching on a sweater front or sleeve. I chose pens in the same fussy way that I chose wooden single-point needles versus circular; I debated over which writing tablet to employ, just as I pondered whether to go twisted rib or plain. I fingered reams of paper for their fiber content. A piece of writing was a tangible thing, with shape and texture and heft. Writing was something I made with my hands, too.

The problem first arose in college, during final exams. I was an English major, and those three-hour exams, sometimes two or three scheduled per day, were essay question after essay question.

I crammed blue books with my frenzy of precision-crafted letters, but after an hour or so my right hand would slowly begin to cramp—I'd put down my pen, try to shake it out, massage my wrist, clench and unclench my fist. Other hyperanxious students in the room did the same, a constant ripple of flapping hands. I'd tell myself it was just tension, loosen my grip on my letters, take a deep breath, and write on. But the time till the onset of cramp grew shorter, less than an hour, half an hour, fifteen minutes. I'd get home in the evening too hand-cramped to knit, and just tell myself my hands had done enough for the day. The day after exams were done I'd devote wholly to knitting, like a reward.

I was also a creative writing major, though, and the longhand writing of stories soon became problematic—a page or two and the ache would start, and distract me from the work. I tried writing shorter stories. I tried switching from short stories to poems. A writer friend showed me I was holding my pen wrong, in too intense a grip, and I tried to modify my clutch. I got by; I wrote in short spurts, taking lots of breaks and trying to flap the ache away. But when the time came to write a novel, I knew something had to change. I finally forced myself to learn to compose on a computer. I mourned the loss of the handcraft involved; no more rustle of paper and scratch of pen, no more tangible feel of *making something*. But I know I couldn't possibly write 300 pages (more like 3,000, really, probably, counting drafts and revision) by hand—certainly not by my aching, betraying hand. It felt so cold and mechanical at first—my style felt cramped, with the most pleasurable aspect of the writing process snatched away—but my fingers finally made friends with the keyboard. I was still *creating*. The letters weren't handcrafted, but at least my hands were still *at work*. The weave of words was still the thing, the stitching together of sentences. Hours and hours of writing at the computer produced a complete novel in three months, only a slight lower back strain and tired eyes; my fingers could still dance all night. I'd won. And the sweaters for friends, the hats and scarves for myself, the woolly baby suits for showers, all the obsessive knitting still merrily clicked along just fine. I went from computer to knitting, back and forth—from a chapter to a sleeve, from the end of a pattern sequence to a new scene, back and forth, victorious, writing and knitting just fine, happily filling up hours, days, years.

Until the cramp came back. This time, while knitting. The faintest ache in my right wrist, recalling the old pen-holding writer's cramp I'd beaten back with a keyboard and mouse. The knitting cramp crept lower down my wrist and forked at the base of my thumb, the knuckle of which began to need regular cracking out of position. I'd put down the needles, try to shake it out, massage my wrist, and clench and unclench my fist. I'd tell myself it was just tension, loosen my stitches, take a deep breath, and knit on. But, again, the time before the onset of cramp grew shorter—now less than an hour, then half an hour, then fifteen minutes. I'd put down the knitting feeling too hand-cramped to write, and I'd just tell myself my hands had done enough for the day. Cramp would retreat when I'd stop, and soon I'd take up arms again. No petty demon of a cramp was going to trounce me.

You're holding the needles wrong, a knitter friend suggested, *you have too intense a grip.*

I tried to be less intense. I tried larger or smaller needles, thicker or finer yarn, tried putting myself on a ten-rows-at-a-time diet: *Put the needles down,* I'd boom at myself every ten minutes, *and back away from the knitting,* but obsessions are deaf to calls for restraint.

And by now I was no longer a creative writing Student; I was a Creative Writing Professor. With thick and endless stacks of student pages to read and comment on, their typed lines needing critique, editing, commentary—so now the pen was back in my hand. I crammed their short stories and novels with my frenzy of precision-crafted letters, and the result was, of course, cramp. The Return of Writing Cramp. It gained ground. I tried to hold the pen differently to write; the result was illegible scrawls. I tried to write less on the page, and include longer typed letters as feedback, but it was too macro a response for my professorial, obsessive, detail-oriented taste. I bought a wrist brace, and it helped, but I hated the way it reshaped my feedback into a foreign, quavering, unfamiliar hand. And I hated the way people said *Oh, you have carpal tunnel?* to me, as if to say *Welcome to the Club!*, meaning *Welcome to a common problem so many of us have to deal with.* And then they'd tell me stories of their carpal-tunnel'd friends, with their physical therapies and surgeries, all of whom seemed to wind up on disability, disabled, somehow unhanded.

No, I'd airily insist, it's just a little cramp.

I didn't want to give it an official, technical name—that would *make* it a problem, make it something I'd *have* to deal with. I was afraid of the words *carpal tunnel,* the words *disability, nerve damage, strain.* The brace felt like a pronouncement of those words, an admission of defeat, a giving in. And I couldn't knit with the brace, either—its Velcro snagged the yarn. I decided to just ignore the cramp. Don't listen to it, don't give in. Don't *let* it be a problem. Queen Elizabeth, I was sure, never yielded to cramp. I bet they had to pry those needles from lifeless Madame Defarge's cold, dead hands. And all those writers throughout history before me, who'd cranked out those epic masterpieces by hand, clutching their whittled quills—if they could stick it out, so would I.

But it isn't working. The Maginot Line of my keyboard and mouse and ergonomic wristpad have given way; cramp has found me there, too, and it takes over both hands now, left and right, after a scant five or ten minutes of work. And it doesn't scuttle away anymore when I stop, but merely dulls out overnight. Cramp has moved in, infiltrated, set up camp. Cramp gets a good rest and is ready to attack first thing the next morning, lying in wait for me at my knitting basket, my desk. Cramp is here to stay.

You should see a doctor, a professor friend tells me.

And what is a doctor going to tell me, I think. *Stop?*

Maybe things aren't that dire. After all, I can *buy* the baby booties and knit caps for presents. I can buy mittens and sweaters and socks. Or, hey, I can buy a knitting machine. What difference does it really make? And I can always speak into a mini-corder, hire someone to type a transcription, or just write one slow sentence at a time. So, I'll slow down. So no more knitting binges that last hours; no more cranking out a novel in three months. So, those days are over. After all, being a writer means getting words onto a page whatever it takes—the

Needle Notes

Does that itchy sweater bother you? To soften it up and reduce itch, wash the sweater with soap (not detergent) and rinse thoroughly; repeat one or two times. Then give the sweater a cream rinse with your favorite hair-conditioning product. Block dry and see if it doesn't feel softer than before. If the itchiness is still a problem, try wearing a silk undershirt between skin and sweater.

ink-stained fingers or the happy, busy clack of keyboard keys are not the real goal, they're just an image of how to get there. But speaking words into a dictaphone suddenly makes it about speech. Words become sound waves, not the beautiful texture of letters, the printed lines of nap and nub so gorgeous to craft. If it's a form of *talking*, is it, still, a piece of writing? Just as a knitting machine becomes about the efficiency of it all, the mass-production stylizing, the homogenizing of each and every stitch. The knitting is taken out of knitting. It becomes mere partnering with a cool, impervious machine, the real maker of the thing to whom you simply offer up the yarn. Something wonderfully personal and messy and primally hands-on gets lost. *To write* and *to knit*; each infinitive will have to lose one definition.

So I'm afraid of *Stop*. I'm even afraid of *Do less*, of *Take a break* or *Just give it a rest*. Of *Slow down*. Idle hands are the Devil's Handmaiden, and I'm not giving in to that Dark Force.

Because I'm the Girl Who Makes Things. I'm the Girl Who Is Good With Her Hands.

But what if I'm not anymore? My hands are looking at retirement. My hands must throw themselves up in the air. My hands don't have it in them to keep doing the things I love, that make me feel special, that make me feel generative, creative, ancestral, that win me *oohs* and applause. I will soon have to let go of something I hold so dear, and that frightens me. How will I keep on loving the hands that can no longer make things? What will I do then? What will I be then? These questions make my stomach, yes, cramp.

I look at my mother's hands now. In recent years the arthritis that her side of the family is famous for has taken over her hands, gnarled them with red bumps, swollen her knuckles, and increased her inability to handle things or make do. She looks at them mournfully—not simply because they ache, but because they're the hands of another person now, a woman she never thought she'd become but now is frightened that she is. Useless. Ugly. Sick. Old. They scare her. She has other things failing and going wrong. She's afraid of something much bigger than what I'm afraid of. I can help her with her earrings, with opening prescriptions and mail, but what I really need to do is hold my mother's hands more often. I need to steer less clear. That is something I can do.

And my father no longer sculpts. He's gotten older and has less stamina for the physical effort involved. While his hands are still beautiful, the hands of a younger man, he now has an essential tremor, a benign but betraying form of palsy, and his beautiful hands shake. He is no longer a sculptor who sculpts, and he's at a loss. I watch him wander the house from room to room, casting about for what to do. I am worried he'll spill that scalding cup of coffee on himself, cut himself with a razor or scissors or vegetable peeler, never mind being able to hold the carving knife. It's getting worse. Some day, perhaps soon, my father will need more help, real help with all the little things that to us are a snap, and I need to be there to lend a hand. That is something I can do.

I need to figure out how to handle things from here. How to deal, create, be useful in ways I'm only just beginning to grapple with or grasp. Make every stitch and every word count, instead of counting every stitch and every word. Find in every mere moment something wonderfully personal and messy, make of every moment something primally hands-on. Redefine what it means to be the Girl Who Is Good With Her Hands.

Tara Ison

Six: Knit One, Purled Together

"We construct a narrative for ourselves, and that's the thread that we follow from one day to the next. People who disintegrate as personalities are the ones who lose that thread."

—PAUL AUSTER

Knitting ties us to others in time-honored ways, yes, but in odd, eccentric, fun ways as well. For *Zen and the Art of Knitting,* I interviewed a knitter who makes sushi and other foodstuffs in three-dimensional knitted representations. She has a great time doing it and is able to make "comfort food" that lasts longer than an evening's meal. Yarn-crafted ham dinners, snack cakes, and platters of spaghetti represent for her the love and warmth we look for in what we knit. As creative people, we can concoct things surprisingly different from conventional sweaters, mittens, and scarves, if we choose.

Stories of less-than-traditional knits explored here include "The Square Truth" by Joanne Catz Hartman. It's the tale of one knitter's inability to craft anything other than square-shaped items—she hasn't mastered other contours yet—and how she finds ways to make those squares hold meaning. Jennifer D. Munro writes of a life that's been blessed by the knitted leis and oddly shaped stuffed animals that her Hawaiian grandmother crafted with love. Though these items aren't the most attractive objects the author ever encountered, they hold all the tenderness and devotion her grandmother meant to express. Cindy Dorn tells of knitting a simple scarf for her niece, recently off to college, and how she was able to create within that scarf a reflection of the tenacity and courage she's encountered in her niece.

Not all knitting need end up as serious items, or be crafted with great skill and dexterity. Sometimes knitting's just a celebration of life, an acknowledgment of the people we love, an appreciation of the ways our lives are intertwined. Create something new with your knitting. Be nontraditional. Let the spirit of inventiveness move through your fingers.

kathleen's scarf

A friend recently offered to teach me to knit. "Would you like to learn?" she asked. She taught me this knitting rhyme: In through the front door, around the back, out through the window, and off jumps Jack.

Now I knit, sort of.

For my first project I've liberated a big ball of bright red yarn that I found in my sewing basket, to knit a scarf for my niece Kathleen. She's leaving Los Angeles to go to college in Boston. I picture her wrapping up in it, covering her head and looping it around her neck as she experiences the shock of her first eastern winter, and longs for family and friends and the furnace winds of Santa Ana.

"Close-knit" is what folks have always called the big family I come from.

I think about that as I knit the scarf, but dropped stitches and gaping holes, uneven rows and bunched up clumps of stitches are what make up the scarf. "Tightly knit" is what I'm after. A perfect scarf.

"What is it?" people ask.

I keep knitting.

I could rip it all out and begin again, but I decide not to. I look at the scarf and feel a surge of pride in its rows of completed stitches, and how much better the new rows are compared to the old ones. I finger the bumpiness of the first rows and peek through the holes, and wonder at the improvement.

Kathleen has had a year much like the scarf: stupefying in its imperfection. As she applies to colleges, graduates from high school, and gets a summer job, her parents have separated and are splitting up. The idea of this marriage as durable and dependable comes completely undone. Kathleen's mother leans on the tight fabric of family and friends, and she emerges shaky but determined.

Kathleen does not unravel.

A trip to the yarn store prods me to change course: a soft scarf made from chenille, to offer comfort; a happy bright scarf made from multicolored thick yarn, to bring cheer; or an expensive cashmere scarf to proclaim her value. But I remain true to the scarf attached to my knitting needles, a bright-red rag of a scarf.

Needle Notes

Does your scarf curl annoyingly? First, block it by dampening it and laying it flat on a towel. If that doesn't do the trick, try lightly steaming the scarf.

With every stitch I think of Kathleen and all that lies ahead for her, and how there's solace in imperfection. Life seems to be a spectrum of relationships, of deep commitments and meaningless encounters and everything in between. And nobody, as the old cliché goes, is perfect.

So we wind our way through, sometimes on our knees, in the dark, feeling the sides of the mineshaft, praying for a mere pinpoint of light. And what we get is compassion for those who crawl behind us, and a better understanding of those who groped ahead.

Other times there's just the joy of it all. The big, sloppy, boundless joy of life. Our reward for sticking it out and not turning away in disillusionment.

I keep knitting and develop a bit of a rhythm. *In through the front door, around the back.* If we're lucky, life is mostly routine. *Out through the window, and off jumps Jack.*

My needles move just like the old pros on the park benches, at PTA meetings, and other places where I have envied knitters forever. How did this happen?

I've come to believe that tightly knit scarves (or families) have little to do with perfection. Close-knit comes from sticking it out through the dropped stitches, gaping holes, the pulling apart and bunching together. You keep going, you carry on. You end up with whole cloth.

All of us in Kathleen's large extended clan hold her in our hearts. As she readies for takeoff she has all she needs for a life of meaningful accomplishment, and some meaningless folly.

I continue to knit the scarf. It's taking shape and reminds me of Kathleen's deep, resilient heart. Her huge, bright-red rag of a heart.

Cindy Dorn

the square truth

🐚 "What are you knitting?" friends and strangers ask when they see me, my size-8 wooden knitting needles in hand, connecting loops, making stitches with my 100-percent-cotton blue thread, the same deep intense color of my young daughter's eyes. Her little friends ask me too. "What are you making? What's it going to be?" I look up from my work and smile, "I'm making a square." Sometimes, though it's really a rectangle. I'm a beginner, a knitting neophyte, and all I've mastered so far in the infancy of my knitting career are four-sided figures.

I do love being mistaken for a real knitter, one who can make more than squares or rectangles, one who might actually know what worsted wool is and what double-pointed needles are for. I get giddy when real knitters use words like "gauge" and "overcast stitch" around me, assuming I'm fluent in their language. But I'm unfamiliar with the tools of the trade, and not well versed in the vocabulary of the language. I'm new to this culture, a visitor with wide eyes trying to take it all in. I have a handful of four-sided, uneven practice squares and rectangles to show for my immersion.

Many hours of practice lay ahead of me before I will blend into the world of yarn and needles and patterns, and more time and learning are necessary before I can apply for my knitting visa.

Knitting came into my life unexpectedly. It was something I'd always wanted to learn; knitting was on my long-term "to-do" list, sitting somewhere between becoming fluent in Spanish and writing the great American novel—something I'd get around to doing one day. That day turned out to be a Wednesday night Beginner Knitting Class. A friend, a well-established knitter, had given me a gift certificate from our local knitting store for the workshop. I would not have signed up on my own. I was a busy mom of a young child, attempting to balance writing and working at preschool, and I read voraciously in any spare time I had left. But the gift certificate had an expiration date; if I were to learn to knit, I had to do it then.

I announced to my husband and daughter that I was going off to learn how to knit that night. "Oh, you can make me things!" my daughter exclaimed. I wasn't so sure. And I was even more unsure when I got there and discovered I was the only true beginner in the class. The others had just forgotten how. Casting on was easy—it reminded me of the finger knitting I had done as a child—but actually knitting with two needles was impossible. I was truly knitting impaired. After much frustration and fumbling with the needles and twisted yarn, and taking up way more than my personal share of the extremely patient instructor's time, something finally clicked, and it wasn't just the knitting needles. My fingers finally did what everyone else's were doing. I was hooked. I also became obsessed.

The needles and yarn became a permanent item among the contents of my handbag, easily accessible to pull out at any opportunity. My works in progress sat on my lap in the car so I could knit at red lights, which, I know, is not the safest idea. But idle time is idle time, and I had to knit. I knit everywhere; at gas stations while filling up, in line at the grocery store. If I arrived at school to pick up my daughter a minute too early I'd sit in the car to knit, and more than once picked her up a little late because I had to, just *had* to finish a row. I knit late into the night, forgoing my reading and any meaningful personal interaction with my husband. With all the intense knitting time, I was getting practice. Lots of it.

It paid off. In my daughter's eyes, I am a creative master. I create things, really useful things, from colorful string. The possibilities of "what's it going to be" are endless. With her help in that depart-ment—creativity that stretches far beyond my own—my knitting repertoire consists of tooth-fairy pouches and sleeping bags, pillows, and rugs for small dolls and stuffed animals. My daughter takes the finished knitted pieces and with the assistance of a roll of Scotch tape makes dollhouse pillows, stuffed with folded tissues. I can make rectangles of any size: "this big, Mommy" and she shows me with her hands, and "this small" as she shows me with her fingers. I experiment with different-sized needles, varying thicknesses of yarn. Mistakes are tolerated, even celebrated: pompons can be glued on dropped stitches and can cover up glaring holes.

I feel good about my new hobby, glad when my daughter asks to watch me knit, which she does so silently, mesmer-ized. I want to know what is registering in the growing folds of her blossoming brain. When she's older, will she remember these moments, watching me knit from her car seat, while I sit in front of her in the driver's seat in a parking lot or in the driveway of our home, my needles moving like a conduc-tor's baton in the air? Perhaps she likes to watch because it seems like magic—a creation appearing before our eyes, the metamorphosis from a single strand of twisted fiber into a tightly woven opaque square.

She asks to help me knit, and knows the difference between knit and purl, which way to place the yarn over the needle. I watch her little fingers wrap the string, her singsong voice saying "string over" for purl and "string under" for knit. She's still too young to master the needles, but one day I'll show her when she asks. I taught her how to finger-knit and it was so much fun that I even taught her classmates and showed off all my squares and rectangles. The boys finger-knit red headbands and stuck feathers into them, and we made many purple bracelets. I don't remember who taught me how to finger-knit when I was young, but I loved the repetitive motion, the long strands, the control I had over tightly or loosely pulled yarn. It came back effortlessly, like riding a bike, that "aha, I remember this now" feeling.

I don't have that feeling yet with real knitting. I knit too tightly, and my stitches are holding on for dear life. I sometimes pry and swear at them as I force my needle through the clenched loop. I'm not yet adept enough to drop my shoulders or avert my eyes; I have to concentrate and focus. My husband loves when I knit while he is driving, because focusing on my new hobby means I'm watching my needles and my stitches and not his driving. It's hard to be a backseat driver with knitting needles in my hand. But, I warn him, one day I'll get so good that I won't need to look at what I'm doing.

Sometimes I have glimpses of that future. When my knitting is going well, it's like having the perfect dance partner, a rhythm and a movement that flows and is never forced. I like the feel of the needles in my hands, the smooth wood, the quiet way the needles slide over each other, working together, pulling apart, the feel of the soft wool on my lap and in my hands. Knitting forces me to slow down, to focus on the thing at hand. It's meditation while still keeping my always-moving hands and fingers occupied. When it's working right, it feels effortless and easy, as if the act of knitting has been laying dormant in my genes and just needed to be tapped.

A friend gives me an idea for my work in progress. "What if you make many identical-sized squares and stitch them together?" she suggests. She doesn't mean connecting my squares with Scotch tape, the way my daughter does, but sewing them together. My friend will show me how. I get excited; I will no longer have to answer "squares" when asked what I'm knitting. I will reveal the big picture: a blanket of squares, a quilt. I can still knit in my comfort zone of making squares, and each one will remind me that tiny steps can create something greater. This may take me years to complete.

The author's daughter, admiring a knitted gift.

I realize now that I might need to venture out past beginner basics class and explore the possibilities beyond quadrilaterals. My daughter has all the rectangles she needs. Her bedroom floor is littered with dollhouse-sized sleeping bags and rugs. I can whip out a tooth-fairy pouch for a friend in no time flat. Today she officially outgrew her need for squares and asked me to knit our dog a skirt, a necklace, and shoes for her paws. My heart raced. I don't know how to do the things she wants. I'll be outed; she'll discover that her mother is not a Real Knitter. But then I thought about what she wanted and relaxed. I may need instruction for the skirt and socks, but a dog collar necklace—I can do that, right? Isn't it just a really long rectangle?

Joanne Catz Hartman

DOG COLLAR PATTERN
BY JOANNE CATZ HARTMAN

This can be used as a dog collar cover—
great for winter.

MATERIALS:
Worsted-weight multicolored yarn
Size 8 needles

PATTERN STITCH: Knit I row, purl I row (stockinette)

INSTRUCTIONS:
Cast on 10 stitches for medium-size dogs—such as a Labrador or other retriever.

Cast on 5 stitches for smaller breeds; 12–15 stitches for larger breeds.

Use dog's neck measurement, or dog collar, as guide for length. Attach with Scotch tape, if you're age five and under; use excess yarn at ends to tie bows.

For fancier collars, make loops and sew on dog-bone-shaped buttons at end to attach.

Cast on fewer stitches for a thinner necklace look. ●

Needle Notes

To make sure that sweaters will fit kids for a long time to come, knit them top-down and a little bit oversized. When the sleeves and body become too short, undo the cast-off edges and lengthen, either with the leftover yarn or a contrasting color, to just the right size.

a knitter in hawaii

A knitter in Hawaii is as pointless as an elevator for a one-story building. There's no use for warm, woolen garments in a tropical climate. Polynesian natives wore no clothes at all for hundreds of years. When they did, they wore wraps of decorative kapa, a pounded mulberry bark. In other words, they wore, literally, paper—a far cry from cable-knit sweaters. Then the modest missionaries arrived and insisted on covering up front and rear. So, although nudity went out of vogue and the muumuu was invented (to the everlasting delight of stout ladies the world over), there was hardly a need for scarves, socks, and blankets. Clothes in paradise were for covering cleavage, not for cutting chills.

So my Tutu (Hawaiian for grandmother) never knit sweaters, caps, or anything particularly useful. She knitted yarn leis that she presented at special occasions. Made of cheap yarn purchased from the corner Woolworth's, they hung all over my room, from bookshelf corners and door handles, collecting dust. Eventually the rich island insect life turned them into dinner, and the leis disintegrated.

In every old family photo, the birthday girl or high school graduate stands smiling, neck draped with a mass of flower garlands, sometimes stacked up past her chin. Many of the leis were strung together from the fragrant plumerias in our backyard, before we got older and learned to equate love with expensive, store-bought leis of rare flowers and intricate designs.

In every snapshot, a plain, yarn necklace peeks out from the heap of vibrant flowers. The yarn lei always came first, Tutu bestowing the customary kiss with a blue or lavender lei. I thought that respect for elders granted her the honor of giving the first lei, but now I wonder if it wasn't shame that made her step forward quickly, so that her plain lei would soon be covered up by the more glorious creations of nature. Living in a government-subsidized apartment, she had no yard in which to grow flowers, and no money to buy the flower leis the tourists shelled out a fortune for. She had a dying husband to care for and no transportation. So she spent hours at home creating "fake" leis. They smelled of her cigarettes and of decay and medicine, the yarn absorbing the odors of her apartment. I thought she gave the leis with pride, but now I think the pride was reserved entirely for us and our accomplishments. She knitted extras for us to give to friends, one of the few things she could give us in abundance, other than love. My friends liked them, because they were different. But I treated them with casual disregard, as if they were nothing special. I have only one yarn lei now, in a faded red resulting from cheap dye; it's stuffed in a box with my Girl Scout sash and wedding garter. I'm grateful for its permanence, whereas none of the "special" flower leis could be preserved.

Tutu also knitted doilies, potholders, doll clothes, plant hangers, and beach bags, and made hats out of Primo beer cans woven together. Meant to block the sun, the hats never fit our heads. I'm sure that some of the things she made were macraméd or crocheted instead of knitted, but to my childish mind they were all the same—Tutu sitting with a bundle of yarn as she watched a full morning of television game shows. She called out answers before the host could finish the question, looking back and forth between her project and the screen. When she discovered a mistake in her knitting, she shouted "Damn!"—the only swear word in her vast vocabulary. She would hold the sorry creation up to the light, then laugh and smack the fake wood laminate table with the peeling corners, which had been purchased, along with all of her furniture, from an old motel going out of business. The table had a hole in the middle from a screw-in lamp no longer in existence. The grandkids spent hours trying to sink marbles through the *puka*, not understanding that it was a point of shame. The table later went to me after I married and moved out, and I was all too happy when I could afford to replace it.

Instead of unraveling the last twenty minutes' worth of work to recover a dropped stitch, Tutu tossed the yarn aside and smoked a cigarette. "I'm *pau*," she said, indicating that she was done. She was in no hurry, as few islanders are.

Bored with scampering under the table to collect the objects I'd aimed successfully through the *puka*, Tutu's swear word thrilled me. It not only meant her attention would now turn to me, but her expletive was a precise word, standing out in the mishmash of foreign words she wove through her English. Like most locals, she peppered her everyday speech with words from Hawaii, China, Japan, Portugal, and the Philippines. The hodgepodge language had been necessary for communication between the migrant workers who came to work the sugar-cane fields. Despite the passage of time, the untidy ends of all this immigration had never been snipped and tucked in, but still remained hanging out of the final project of Hawaii's melting pot, waving in the trade winds.

Tutu was raised on the sleepy island of Kauai in the early 1900s, on a sugar plantation where her father was head carpenter. A first-generation islander descended from a Nordic clan, knitting was in her blood, and she spent her life battling the fact that her inherited craft was largely useless after the family emigrated nearer the equator. Further complicated by the fact that her Norwegian ancestors had crossbred their ice-tolerant genes with fiery Portuguese blood, her struggle was also an inner battle between Arctic and Mediterranean extremes—which perhaps explained why nothing she created ever turned out right. Squares were warped, as if the two poles inside of her pulled her, and her craft, in opposite directions.

Each lopsided square symbolized a warring past and present, not only for Tutu, but for the islands themselves. The last sugar-cane plantation is now gone from my home island of Oahu, where Tutu spent her adult life. The island has been paved over, and sweaters, once a superfluous fashion accessory, are now a necessity in the air-conditioned buildings that spear the downtown Honolulu skyline.

Tutu is gone. Although I might look odd, just as I did as a child, I would prefer one of her asymmetrical ponchos to the store-bought, machine-made sweater on the back of my office chair. I adored the tasseled creations, although they were entirely unnecessary in year-round summer. I wore them in all weather, even to the beach, and never could shake all of the sand out of them. Inspired by Marcia

Brady in the 1970s—I watched her every week on our small black-and-white, wishing my life were more like hers—I looked weird rather than cool, but I didn't know it back then. The ponchos emphasized the fact that I didn't fit in, any more than the other *haole* kids did at my school. I looked less "cool hippie" and more simply strange.

I liked the ponchos not only because I thought they would help me fit in with Marcia's "mainland" life better, but also because the loose drape of yarn covered my chubby body. Ballooning into pubescence, I was glad the missionaries had instituted a climate of full coverage. Tutu once knit me a yellow bikini with red stripes, with one for Barbie to match, but I wore it about as often as the other kids would have worn one of my woven tents. The bikini was more for stylish sunbathing than for swimming, but I wanted my body covered rather than exposed. My white bulges didn't look anything like the lithe brown bodies on the other kids. I was as happy as any tired matron for a closet of muumuus and ponchos.

Tutu made me a tightly knit, oversized yellow poncho, an orange poncho with white stripes, and an airy, red poncho of interlocking flowers. One morning I ran down the aisle of the school bus, heading toward an empty seat at the back. A Hawaiian boy strummed his ukulele as the bus climbed the steep and narrow mountain road with a grinding of gears, picking up scrappy kids as the trade wind kicked up

Needle Notes

Don't be afraid to make something without a pattern. Play with the yarn. See what colors call to you. Give birth to a belt or headband, fashion a wall hanging of your favorite yarn, knit to enjoy the texture and fun. You might be surprised by what you invent. For color fun, try knitting with two strands at once: use one strand of a knitting yarn and pair it with one strand of sewing thread in a contrasting color. Play with the colors. Try a metallic thread and see what happens.

red dirt around them. The ukulele neck stuck out into the aisle as the boy sang, the wind through the open windows carrying his song. My poncho snared a tuning key as I ran past. The ukulele flew from his grasp and bounced down the aisle behind me, like a caught fish flapping on a line, with a discordant, twanging protest that sounded worse than his shouts. The ukulele was unharmed, but my sore *okole* wasn't after he was through with me.

I grew up and the ponchos became the domain of the family dog, named Poncho. He snapped at anyone who tried to steal his hand-me-down blankets, and only Tutu had the courage to take them from him for the occasional washing.

What my Tutu couldn't know was that her final knitting project was as useless as most of what she knit throughout her life. While I was away at college, she spent her last days furiously knitting her last creation. Cigarettes and ashtray replaced by oxygen tank and nicotine gum, she knitted stuffed animals for her great-grandchildren, whom she knew she wouldn't live to see. With no money or possessions to pass on, she wanted a personal legacy to give them.

When I returned home after Tutu died, my mother showed me a collection of misshapen, malformed creatures suffocating in a giant plastic bag. "She wanted your kids to have them," Mom said, her eyes watering. She pulled the odd assortment of unidentifiable animals out one by one. Only when we dared to meet each other's eyes did we laugh, crying at the same time. Tutu had left the perfect gift. I can hear her wheezing laugh, her "Damn!" and the smack of her hand on the table. But this time she didn't have time to set the project aside, to unravel the mistakes and start over. Her second try was often as unsuccessful as the first, anyway, so she didn't bother. She had to keep going, just as she did in life.

My father often calls Tutu's side of the family "stubborn." I call it persistence. She forged ahead with the knitting, like so many failed projects in her life: her marriage to an alcoholic, which she maintained, like so many women of her time, for the sake of the kids. This drunken man slept through the bombing of Pearl Harbor, not far from their bedroom window. She persevered through the trials of a mother who deserted her, and through subsidized housing, food banks, and food coupons—a small reward for a life of hard work. She wore dentures that never fit, made pancakes for her kids when there was no butter or syrup, and endlessly babysat the grandkids while my parents worked days and nights to support us.

Through it all she crafted—my Raggedy Ann doll, my Kanga, Roo, and Eeyore dolls, my Barbie clothes, and my beloved ponchos—because homemade was the most affordable way to go, not because she wouldn't have preferred to give her kids and grandkids china dolls of great beauty or because she needed a hobby to fill her time. She couldn't afford the beautiful yarns I see in stores now, hand-dyed silks and wools of varying hues, a pleasure to behold and touch, works of art before knitters transform the strands into objects with purpose. Her skeins were purchased from the Woolworth's store, now gone, across the street from her tiny Waikiki apartment. My mother and uncle bought her a purebred poodle and a small condo in her final years. Still, these stuffed animals were woven from inexpensive yarn. Tutu didn't know how to splurge.

Mom and I spread the animals out on my parents' bed, covered with Mom's electric blanket. After sixty years of temperate island life, she swears the Ice Age is coming and turns on the heat if the temperature drops into the six-ties. Just as I wish for one of my old ponchos, I'm sure she wishes that Tutu had knitted her a blanket, even an imperfect one.

Mom and I guessed at what each animal was supposed to be. Some were a toss up: dog or horse? bunny or beaver? Tutu had woven them in all the colors of our daily Hawaiian rainbows, so realistic coloring didn't help us identify species. Neither could we depend upon the relative size of ears, or the shape of noses or bodies. Pro-portions were amiss in almost all of them. But the knitting rows themselves were perfect, straight and even.

No stuffing peeked through. All of the ends were tidily snipped and hidden. The patterns stymied her, but she had finally mastered the stitches.

I chose one to take back to college with me, a pink and white elephant, though I had no boyfriend and no plans to start a family anytime soon. The elephant sleeps serenely, with floppy ears, a cute little tail, and a sweet face. The nose flares at the end rather than tapers, and looks more like a long anteater snout than an actual trunk. Still, its genus is unmistakable. I tucked the elephant into the box with my Girl Scout sash and graduation tassels.

When I learned of my first pregnancy years later, the first thing I did was pull the elephant out. The pregnancy ended, and the elephant went back into the box. Several miscarriages later, I didn't pull the elephant out when my next pregnancy was confirmed. I feared the elephant was a curse rather than a good luck charm. I had once wor-ried that when the time came, I selfishly wouldn't be able to give the elephant to the child it was meant for. I wanted it to remain perfect. A child would soil it, gnaw on it, love it to a frayed wad of stuffing. The elephant was too precious, though Tutu had always meant it for that child and not for me. Now it appears that the elephant will always stay as well preserved as a museum piece. When I take it out of the box from time to time, I think not only of Tutu, but of the lost babies.

Tutu kept on laughing even when she could hardly breathe. She would have scoffed at the irony of her last futile project. If there had been time, she would have tried again, and she would have told me to do the same. And, yet, a pink elephant meant for a great-grandchild who will never exist *is* necessary. As necessary as a warm poncho for a shy girl who didn't fit in. As necessary as a yarn lei that will never wither. As necessary as memory, which helps us to keep going. In her final days, Tutu looked to the future, as I now look to the past. She had to work her yarn and needles around the hose to her oxygen tank, a hassle that I'm sure provoked a few "damns," but she didn't let past failures stop her. She forged ahead. An elephant has a long memory, and he'll help me to remember: my grandmother, my babies, the vanished Hawaii of my youth and Tutu's youth. The elephant from now on will sit on a shelf, where it will grow dusty and fade, not sealed in a box where nothing can touch it. He'll prod me to never give up, despite imperfect creations and imperfect life. He'll remind me to laugh, even when it hurts.

Jennifer D. Munro

Seven: For the Love of Yarn

"The painter . . . does not fit the paints to the world. He most certainly does not fit the world to himself. He fits himself to the paint. The self is the servant who bears the paintbox and its inherited contents."

—ANNIE DILLARD

There's nothing that thrills a knitter's sense of aesthetic joy more than the experience of working with rich, sensual fibers: the feeling of a bodily connection to the fiber as it moves through fingers, the fulfilling clack, clack, clack of favorite needles as they ply that fiber. The delight and exuberant celebration of fiber is an irresistible aspect of knitting.

There are fibers for all tastes. Some might use the word "rich" to define fibers that are drenched in gorgeous jewel tones; others might use the word to describe the interplay of the host of colors chosen for a particular work, one shade flattering the next. Others might point to an undyed fiber, beautifully raw and filled with intrinsic animalness, as the most rich and filling sensory experience. Still others find the "fun" fibers—alive with thick slubs, say, or eyelash strands, metallic shimmers, or funky microfibers—to be the best thing to knit.

Close your eyes at your favorite yarn store one day and listen. *Oohs* and *aahs* fill the air as knitters move row by row, first taking in the fibers with their eyes, then picking them up, rubbing them against a cheek, inhaling the scents. Knitting is a craft that fills all the senses, that reminds us of our senses' ability to provide pleasure, inviting us to reconnect physically with the clothes we wear and the things we do with our hands.

Be aware of the fibers you choose, and why you choose them. What element appeals to you about that choice? In what realm of your delightfully creative psyche does that fiber fill a need, a desire, a hunger for connection to the world around you? If there are fibers you've always wanted to try—I dreamed about cashmere for years, afraid to make the leap—seize the day, and try the fiber. Life is too short to never experience the fine sweetness of alpaca gliding through your fingers, the level simplicity of cotton, the spring of wool in which you find bits of hay that stuck to the sheep's coat. Life is a banquet for the senses, and knitting is one of the greatest ways I know to refocus our perspective—to see, feel, and smell anew the gifts of the earth. Indulge in a fiber you've never tried before. This is the day!

it's not the knit,
it's the notion

For me the words "knitting" or "yarn" don't conjure images of grandmothers, sweaters, babies' socks, or Ariadne's Thread, but of my dad. On the face of it, this is astounding because my dad has never knitted a stitch in his life.

It all started when my mother remarried when I was nine. The man I call "Dad" owned Bauman's Notions Store in Manhattan on Second Avenue and 84th Street. He grew up a Jew in this neighborhood, which even in the late 1960s was still called Yorkville and was a mostly German working-class area squeezed between the chic streets of Park Avenue and East End. A notions store, for those who don't know (and I didn't before my mother married into the business), sold fabric, thread, needles, and all kinds of stuff to all the tailors. The store was old and musty, dark and colorless. It hadn't been redone since before WWII. My dad took it over from his father and earned the insubstantial sum of 6,500 bucks a year. My mother, a businesswoman on the way to becoming a success in the advertising world, had other, um, notions. So, in their first joint venture, they decided to take over the adjacent store and open a knitting salon. This seemed odd to me even then, because my dad is a guy's guy. His demeanor is that Fifties-cool slicked-back-hair Sinatra–Tony Curtis kind; the attitude, sardonic Jerry Orbach. He spent his time in Tuesday-night poker games, fixing things, doing whatever guys do with cars, and hanging out with his friends Ted, Pete, Stan, and Roger. All married men, but still their own little Rat Pack.

Still, urged on by my mom, he optimistically and meticulously went ahead with this new venture. They broke through the back wall and made a small space so you could walk from store to store just by passing through a curtain. They installed shiny new floors and bright lights. Along the broken wall, which measured more than 30 feet long and 12 feet high, were dozens of empty bins. While the construction was going on, and no one else was around, my dad and I tossed a little football down the long, narrow store. A couple of times I brought a friend with me from Flushing, where we then lived. We both pretended to be Errol Flynn in *Captain Blood*—no one wanted to be Basil Rathbone—and used the needles, which were now being stocked, as swords. We persuaded my dad to let us go eat at the White Castle because we loved the burgers, and also because that's where the local streetwalkers hung out.

One Saturday, after the construction was finished and the store opened, I drove into the city with my dad. We entered through his old store. We walked to the back and I peeked through the curtain. Clair, who ran the new knitting store, was already doing her Saturday morning deal. Though very German, Clair yentaed around the table with her needles and yarn. I listened to the clatter of voices, the smell of smoke and heavy perfume. My eyes searched vainly for young babes. My dad came back and he and I slipped through the curtain into the knitting store. He mumbled an uncomfortable hello and quickly disappeared back to his familiar dark haunt.

I stayed in the new store and gazed up at those once-empty bins—now a wall of fantastic colors like I'd never seen before in my life. Rows of reds and pinks and blues and grays and greens—so many shades burst out from the wall, from floor to ceiling. I didn't say anything to anyone about it; not then, not ever until now. I just stared. I was in Hebrew school at the time, a mostly lamentable experience, and I was reminded of the story of Joseph and his brothers—so, I thought, *that's* what's this coat of many colors business is all about.

I secretly spent the day going into the store looking at all those colors. I was like Kafka's dog, who one day looks up to find a whole new world. Only it would be many years before I would understand this world of color and its possibilities, years before I would ever go to an art museum; and many more years before I would begin writing down my notions about art. But that day I kept sneaking into the new store and looking up, marveling at all those colors.

The day is memorable for me not only for the colors but also because I rarely went into the city after that. Saturdays were too precious. And soon the store—well, let's just say it wasn't a magic thread leading to financial paradise. My dad ended up getting into a business that suited him better. He bought a small car-parking garage at 86th and First. He began leaving at 5 A.M. every day to make the trek in from Flushing, and then had to park cars all day, but he seemed so much happier.

Ray, an old friend of my dad's who owned the fruit store on the corner, took over the old stores. Ray opened a five-and-dime-type store there to compete with Woolworth's on 86th Street. It turned out that some of the Five and Dime items he sold were bags of dope, which, one morning, led to the store's sudden demise. For some time the stores remained closed. Then the neighborhood began to change, and in moved a middling Yuppie restaurant, the Wicked Wolf. Although I then lived in a cheap walkup apartment on 89th Street, and passed the restaurant countless times, I couldn't bring myself to go inside.

Not that many years ago, when I went back to New York on a visit from my present home of L.A., I made a point of strolling past the old store. A très hip, deep-pocket restaurant now inhabited the space. For the first time in decades, shoulders hunched, I slinked inside. Once again, it was dimly lit. Only now you'd call it "atmosphere." The maitre d' came up to me and asked, a bit snootily, if I wanted to sit at the table or the bar. "Neither," I said, "just looking. My dad used to own a knitting store in this space. Thirty years ago."

"Might be a good business now." He smiled, suddenly friendly. "You sure you don't want a drink? On the house."

I took a seat at the bar and ordered a vodka and tonic.

I stared back in time at the wall behind the bar that once separated the two stores, now mirrored and with a shelf that held scores of differently colored bottles of alcohol. But that's not what I saw, because no matter that I now often write about art—and I've been to hundreds of shows in galleries and museums and art has changed my life—nothing ever opened my eyes to the possibilities of color like the great wall of colored yarn.

Bruce Bauman

Fifteen-Yarn Sweater
by Karen Damskey and Leslie Stormon

The piece uses 1 ball each of 85 yards or more of fourteen different yarns, and 2 balls of the fifteenth. The weights can be mingled, because the needle size and the fact that the pattern is only two rows of any particular fiber controls the sizing. The bulk of your choices should be worsted weight, although ribbons and fine mohairs also work. Whatever yarn you choose for the rib, you will need 2 balls of it.

Some suggestions: Anny Blatt's Berlingot, Sulky, and Muguet; Bouton D'Or's Mutine, Opale, and Organdi; Filatura di Crosa's Cosmos, Rialto, Rittrato, Pom Poms, and Bacci; Noro's Silk Garden, Kuryeon.

MATERIALS:

1 each of 14 different yarns; 2 each of the 15th color, which you'll use as the trim. Fill in your choices below.

1 _____	8 _____
2 _____	9 _____
3 _____	10 _____
4 _____	11 _____
5 _____	12 _____
6 _____	13 _____
7 _____	14 _____

15 _____

3 buttons, to complement your yarns

Sizes 10½ (metric 7) and 8 (metric 5) needles

Sizes	Bust	Length	Sleeve Length
XSM	36"	18"	17"
SM	38"	19"	17½"
MED	40"	20"	17½"
LG	43"	21"	18"
XLG	45"	22"	18" (will require extra yarn)

GAUGE: 3½ sts and 4 rows to the inch

NOTE: Be sure your gauge is correct before starting the garment. If different, go up or down needle sizes to obtain the correct one.

PATTERN STITCH: Multiple of 4 + 3

Row 1 (Right Side): Knit.

Row 2: Purl.

Row 3: K3, *sl1 wyib (with yarn in back), K3, repeat from *.

Row 4: P3,* sl 1 wyif (with yarn in front), p3; rep from *.

Row 5: K1,* sl 1 wyib, K3, repeat from *, end sl, k1.

Row 6: K1,* sl 1 wyif, K3 rep from * end sl, k1.

Rows 7 and 8: Repeat rows 3 and 4.

Row 9: Repeat row 5.

Row 10: P1, *sl 1 wyif, p3; rep from *, end sl1, p1.

BACK: With #10½ needles or size to give gauge and 1st color in progression, cast on 63 (67, 71, 75) 79 sts and beginning with row 2 of pattern st, complete this row, then change to color 2 in progression and work rows 3 and 4, then change to color 3 and work rows 5 and 6. Continue in this manner, repeating pattern and progression until pc measures 10 (10½", 11½", 12") 12½".

SHAPE ARMHOLES AND BACK NECK: Bind off 4 sts the beg of the next 2 rows, then dec I st each side every other row 4 (4, 4, 6) 8 times. When armholes measure 7" (7½", 7½", 8") 8½", shape back neck: Bind off center 17 (19, 19, 21) 23 sts, then dec I st each side of neck every other row twice. When armholes measure 8 (8½", 8 ½", 9") 9½", bind off.

FRONTS: Work 2 to correspond. With #10½ needles and first color of progression, cast on 31 (33, 35, 39) 39 sts and work as for back until armholes measure 6" (6½", 6½", 7") 7½".

SHAPE NECK: Bind off 4 (4, 4, 5) 5 sts at front neck edge once, then bind off 2 sts the beg of the next neck edge row 2 (2, 2, 2) 3 times, then dec I st at neck edge row 2 (3, 3, 3) 2 once. When fronts match back in length, bind off.

FINISHING: Lightly steam all pieces. Weave or serge all ends securely. With color chosen for trim and #8 needles with right side facing, pick up sts along bottom edges of sleeves and work in reverse st st for I"; bind off on the knit side. Sew shoulder seams. Sew side seams and sleeve seams. Set sleeves into armholes. With #8 needles and trim yarn and right side facing, pick up sts along bottom edge of jacket and work in reverse st for I", bind off on the knit side. Work neck edge in same manner, then work front bands in same way spacing 3 buttonholes into first row of trim on right front band. ●

"Without having experienced the cold of winter, one cannot appreciate the warmth of spring."

—CHINESE PROVERB

knit think

When I am knitting, I am not thinking about not-knitting things I ought to be doing (there are always not-knitting things I ought to be doing). I am not thinking about things I will shortly be doing or things I have recently done. When I am knitting, I am not thinking about writing or parenting or eating or time or housework or money or any of the other things that normally keep my mind racing at top speed from morning until late, late at night.

When I am knitting, I am thinking about *knitting*. Sometimes it's the project of the moment—I like to tweak and alter patterns to suit myself, and because I am still a semi-novice knitter I need to concentrate to make sure the sweater is not turning into a scarf or the hat into a pair of mittens. As I cast on, I debate slimming the body, making the fit a little closer. How many extra stitches do I cast on to add two cables down the front? Well, that depends on how thick the cables are . . . how about wandering cables? How about an all-over pattern stitch? As I progress, I consider my options: Should I widen the neck? Lengthen the sleeves or remove them altogether? I could use a three-needle bind-off instead of sewing up—I hate sewing up. Then again, I might just rip it all out and start over without the ribbing at the bottom.

While all this bubbles away on the front burner, the pots on the back burner simmer gently, not requiring my immediate attention. I think about things like being a single mother yet again, and how these never-ending changes affect my young daughter. What am I teaching her about relationships? They are not permanent; people can leave and not come back. Love can change, in what looks like a split second, to not-love. I am not thinking of myself, alone again at thirty-four, and what it might mean that I can't seem to settle down and make anything work with anyone. Is it a bad thing? Is it an okay thing? Am I going to be on my own for the rest of my life? Do I want to be alone for the rest of my life? I knit, and I don't worry.

If the knitting in hand is not obsessing me (the dreaded "dud project"), I contemplate other projects I have going on. For instance, while up to my elbows in a deeply boring napkin/placemat/dishcloth set (a gift that needed to be done—on a *schedule* no less) I mentally occupied myself with daydreams of projects currently "on hold," because of course I usually have five or six going at any one time. (Are there people who don't do this? I can't even imagine.) Thoughts of my daughter's cabled cardigan, a pair of new mittens in soft wool, a couple of beautiful baby buntings and my first Fair Isle socks brought me safely to the other side of stockinette-stitch purgatory—without impaling myself on my needles or throttling myself with my yarn.

Two sticks and a string are my ticket to a vacation from motherhood. If I am not knitting and my daughter is elsewhere, she is still present. There are, of course, the small-scale worries of the moment: "Is she okay? Is she eating? Are those silly party shoes she put on this morning giving her blisters? Is she having fun? What am I going to give her for dinner? Should I sign her up for ballet?" And then there are the more sizable worries: "Am I not spending enough time with her? Does she feel neglected when I am always distracted, tired, working? Is she sad that we don't live with Daddy? Is she angry? Will she be angry someday? Is she well adjusted? Does she know I love her?" But in that knitting place there are no meals to be planned, permission slips to remember to sign, play date organizing calls, school forms to fill out, work schedules requiring adjustment, and child care to arrange. No panics about saving up for the years of therapy that being my daughter is eventually going to require. I am on an island. I *am* an island.

Suzanne's daughter, in a cozy spot.

When I am knitting, I am on the ground. I am grounded. I can feel the roots of my body spreading into the earth. My breathing slows, evens. My hands repeat a motion again, again, again, and my mind is wandering through my stash, picking up and putting down hanks and balls and skeins. I am envisioning swatches—how would a sweater in this worsted wool look with a collar of fur? If I knitted this fiery red glittery stuff and this pink eyelash together on size 13 needles, would that be a fun shawl, maybe? What would the drape be like? Do I want to relax with a purple mohair scarf, snuggle down with mauve mittens? How about a passel of hats for Christmas (it *is* already August)? Is this chunky variegated yarn too busy to use with cables? Should I just keep it simple and let the yarn speak for itself? I have this lovely fine mohair-y stuff from the thrift store . . . a fluffy ballerina wrap sweater for my daughter? A hipster beret for my sister?

Money fears dissolve as I mentally survey the wealth of a stash accumulated through single-minded scourings of sale bins, thrift stores, yard sales. Redesigns of patterns to accommodate yarn substitutions keep my mind off the dwindling bank account, the papers to sign for assistance of various types, the humiliating meetings with "workers" to determine if I am poor enough for help. Those perpetual concerns about taking days off when my daughter is sick, and what that might mean at the end of the month, go to find some other single mother to harass for a while. I knit my daughter a sweater to keep her warm, and turn down the thermostat a little with a half-done afghan across my knees.

I remember my mother unraveling sweaters from the Salvation Army Free Box to make things to keep us warm, too, and those projects must have done the same things for her as they do for me.

Time, while my hands are busy, is only time. Not time to fill when I am lonely and insomniac and the nights are long, not time scraped up at the end of the day to spend with my girl before she goes to bed, and not time wasted resentfully waiting for this thing or that thing. I pick up yarn and needles, and the ten minutes between arriving for an appointment and the appointment itself become ten minutes to rejuvenate myself, to steady anxious nerves while I watch whatever it is grow between my fingers, the ball of yarn in my knitting bag turning and turning. I carry my serenity with me. An evening flies by as my wooden needles click softly and comfortably in the silence of a sleeping house while I double-check for dropped stitches to pick up, loose stitches needing a tug, buttonholes to adjust, errors to rip back. I am quiet-minded, busy-handed. My daughter is sleeping safely in her room, and I don't have to go anywhere to find this.

Suzanne M. Cody

when you knit my sweater

When you knit my sweater,
leave some holes, some knobby nubs.
I want to see where your hands have been.
I don't want anyone to think a machine
has knit this, don't want anyone to think
it came from a store. I want you to breathe
through the gaps in the wool, want your knuckles
to bulge at the collar, the hem. I want to feel
your knit and purl like an inhale and exhale,
surrounding me with the heat from your lungs,
wrapping me like a fly in the perfect,
imperfect, spiderweb silk of your love.

Gayle Brandeis

if these yarns could speak

I like to knit with recycled yarns, yarns with a history. The yarn I am now knitting with was once a beautiful sari, the traditional flowing robe of women from an exotic faraway land. In fact, originally it was a very fine silk thread, woven into the fabric that made up the robes worn by women in India and Nepal. This is an area with some 500 million women who wear saris every day of their lives. Have you ever tried to wear a sari? It's not as easy as it looks. It's made up of 10 meters of cloth, which you wrap around and around yourself, until there is just enough fabric left to cover your shoulders, head, and occasionally your face. I guess I just wasn't cut out for sari wearing. Let's face it: There is nothing elegant about tugging and grabbing at your clothes so they don't fall off. But for these women, it is the most natural thing in the world.

In India and Nepal the women wear saris when they shop in the marketplace, care for their children, tend their gardens, and wash their dishes. They wear finer saris when they go to weddings and funerals and take sacred ritual baths in the River Ganges. On special holy days they wear elegant golden embroidered saris. These robes are worn over and over until the day they are given up for recycling.

Each time the yarn changes color I am reminded of all the different saris that are used to make each skein. I recall what I know of the traditional colors of saris: red for weddings; white for cremation ceremonies; saffron orange and gold for temple holy days; and pink, blue, and green for everyday wear. As I come upon four inches of ruby red I imagine that it must have been part of a sari that was worn at a wedding. Whose wedding was it? Was it an arranged marriage? Was it a marriage of love and happiness? Were there children? As I knit further I come across a golden sparkling thread. How many sacred prayers were said while wearing this sari? How many were prayers for peace, health, and the happiness of loved ones?

I find myself questioning what reason someone might have for discarding a sari. Did it go out of fashion because the color was "just so last year"? Or did it get torn while tending chores, chopping wood, or carrying water? I don't know; but what I do know is that saris are traded for new ones or sold by weight to vendors who travel through the villages. Once those saris are collected, they are separated by fiber: synthetics from natural fibers and cotton from silk. The silk is specially processed to make the most beautiful yarn I've ever seen.

The process is similar to recycling boxes or paper. All the silk saris are thrown into a huge grinder, which rips up the garments until they are reduced to threads. The fiber is sold by the bag in 50-kilo sacks of multicolored "fluff" to a woman's cooperative in a remote village in Southern Nepal. The shelter that spins this fiber into yarn offers shelter to approximately seventy-five women who have as many stories to tell about their past as the saris that they recycle.

When I visited this cooperative, one woman told me of how she had been married at age fourteen to a man whom she had never met before the wedding. Her heart belonged to another, but her family did not agree with the union. The man they chose for her had diabetes, and, to make matters worse, he was an alcoholic. She bore him two children, both daughters. Amazingly, in many parts of the world it is still considered a woman's duty to produce a son who can carry on the family name. Although she did her best to take care of her husband's health by encouraging him to eat properly and to quit drinking alcohol, he would not listen. He died from diabetic complications when her children were only six and eight years old. As she had not birthed a son, her in-laws decided she must have bad luck, or "bad karma" as they say. Not wishing any more bad fortune to befall the family, they sent her and her children away. She came to the women's shelter with a strong intention to make a better life for herself and her children.

Like many women who find themselves at the shelter, she is a survivor. The shelter provides a temporary safe house for women and children who have been abandoned or have escaped abusive situations. Here in the shelter, women are taught to spin yarn, a skill that earns them a good living. This simple cottage industry gives an opportunity for better living conditions for themselves and their children. Most women quickly move

Needle Notes

Are you allergic to wool? Many people who think they are allergic are actually experiencing contact dermatitis due to the wool's itchiness or due to dyes and other chemical agents used in processing the wool. To find out if you're really allergic, knit up a small swatch and pin it to your underwear for a few hours. If the skin breaks out, you're allergic. If it doesn't, you're just irritated and might be able to find a different wool, perhaps one less chemically processed, that you can wear.

into homes of their own and are able to send their children to private schools, where they will have an education that offers greater opportunities.

Each day women come to the shelter to collect supplies and to drop off finished yarn. No one is excluded. Every woman does her part to help with the process. Those who cannot spin yarn are busy washing the already processed yarn with soap and softener and then hanging the yarn in the sun to dry, while others attach labels and weigh the skeins. It is very rewarding to see the changes that the women undergo when they regain self-respect and hope. The women may come to the shelter emotionally fragile, but within days they are singing and laughing together. It isn't difficult to see how spinning fragments of fiber into beautiful yarn helps these women weave dignity and inner strength into their own lives.

"Pass the synthetic yarn department, then, with your nose in the air."
—ELIZABETH ZIMMERMAN, *Knitter's Almanac*

As I knit here in my garden in California, I remember the women I have come to know and love who live in that faraway land. Women who move through the marketplace, as graceful as goddesses wrapped in silk saris. I think about the women who have shredded and respun the fiber, and I think of others like myself who will knit with this unusual yarn. We knit sweaters and scarves for friends, families, and for ourselves. We knit blankets for new babies and grandchildren. We knit to create beauty and to express our spirit. Most of all we knit because it connects us to our source and one another.

But the legacy doesn't end here. It lives on with each creation that is made. Where will it go? Will it be handed down through the generations of mother to daughter? Will the same silk thread that was once worn while tending a baby in Asia now be made into a blanket that warms a child in another part of the world?

Oh, if these threads could talk! We would learn of many generations of women in all parts of the world. We would hear their histories, their stories, and their gifts. We would see the deeper connection, which binds all people, of all nations. I believe that ultimately it would tell us how truly similar we all are. It would tell how we all love our families, shed tears when we are hurt, and how our hearts expand when we feel the grace of God's creations. We would see that we all have the same innate desire to create and connect and share love. We would be less concerned with what separates us, and more interested in that which connects us.

Yes, there are many colors in each skein, but the thread I am the most aware of is the invisible thread that connects us all.

Amana Nova

Eight: Knitting Through Grief, Back to Life

"After desolation, grief brings back our humanity."

—MASON COOLEY

*L*ook at what knitting actually is, for a moment. It's the plying of a strand of yarn, making loose connections within the strand. None is so tight as to be considered a knot, and yet the resulting weave is usually strong enough to withstand a lifetime of wear. In this magic of coherence, we find an echo of the experience of grief: What feels so heartbreakingly solitary, existential, and drawn out eventually joins us together with others. An experience in which we feel separate and disjointed slowly evolves until we are part of a greater whole. A time of mourning, in which everything may appear futile and fruitless, eventually fuses into something larger than the experience of loss, just as a knitted thing becomes more than the single thread itself.

But like knitting, grief is a slow process. If we try to rush ourselves through it, we'll get the same inadequate results we'd expect
if we rushed and cut corners on a knitting project. Ideally, knitting
has taught each of us to be patient with a work in process. When
grief finds its season in your life (and no life is exempt), be as patient
with yourself as you'd be with a very complicated knitting project.
Go slow. Indulge in quietness. Allow yourself to lie fallow until the
seeds of a new season are ready to bud. Feel deeply, and trust that
the ache now permeating your bones, your breathing, your very
skin, will lessen day by day, just as you know a sweater grows day by
day. To everything, there is a season.

"I ignored many of the rules that seemed to paralyse most knitters into sticking
to monochrome garments. Merrily, I combined colours and textured yarns,
made knots in the middle of rows, and used up to twenty colors in a single row.
. . . Playing with this most wonderful fabric, I poured every influence I encountered into it—tiled floors, ancient walls, carpets, early maps were all turned
into knitting designs."

—KAFFE FASSETT, *Glorious Knits*

why i knit

🐚 Dear Editor,

Hi, I heard about the essay contest for your book from my teacher Mrs. Mott. She teaches kids how to knit so they have fun hobbies to do after school or when they are bored.

I am thirteen-and-a-half years old and will be in the eighth grade this school year. We are going to start a new project this year. We are going to learn how to circle knit. We will make knitted caps for babies that are premature at the hospital.

I started knitting in the fourth grade. My teacher taught me to knit because she wanted me to make little squares for a big blanket for older people. We went to Wal-Mart to put the squares together.

When I started knitting and making stuff for other people, I was happy. Making stuff for others is fun for me. I know they will like what I make a lot.

Some people, when they get stuff other people have made for them, are happy. They are happy that someone else is thinking of them and not just thinking about themselves.

They might use the blanket we made to cover up with. It's nice to have something someone else has made. When other people make stuff, it might be cherished forever. That is what makes other people happy.

I stopped knitting because I had to go back to my mom and dad's house. At their house there were lots of problems, so I stopped knitting. With all the problems I had no time to knit.

I started knitting again in the sixth grade because I needed something to do. At that time most of the problems stopped. Knitting is a fun craft to do any time of the day.

Some of the projects I like to do are to make parts of things, like a big blanket, or to make a baby pillow, baby blanket, doll pillow, and a cat beanbag. The baby blanket and pillow are for my cousin who is only five months old. The beanbag was my first project.

My teacher Mrs. Mott helps me make most of these projects. This is a fun activity. She showed me how to purl. Purl for a pillow and it is easy to do.

Thank you,
Bekka Gnewikow

Rebecca (Bekka) Gnewikow

the red guernsey

⅚ When you start the Fisherman Pullover for Advanced Knitters, dismissing the daunting appearance of its complex patterns and the tiny gauge—31 stitches and 43 rows to 4 inches—you know perfectly well you're not an advanced knitter. It's the hardest pattern you've ever tackled. And besides, it'll take forever. Years, probably. But . . . well, you think, how hard can it be? One stitch at a time. Like walking. Knit, purl, yarn over, cables, increase, decrease. Just basics. And you can always ask for help.

Using US 1 circular needles, cast on 320 stitches. Work k1p1 rib for 2 inches.

Miscarry.

Again.

Change to US 2 circular needles and increase evenly over round to 352 stitches. Change doctor, diet, job, gym, hairstyle, housekeeper. Begin pattern Chart A (three times: you keep losing count until you resort to markers to set off each panel).

When you learn of the other woman, imagine dropping your

wedding ring down the sewer or the garbage disposal (everyone imagines that), but better: imagine burning the red Guernsey you thought you were knitting for your husband. The wool, though, is so beautiful—all the way from Scotland, as is this intricate pattern—and you've already put so much love and work into it. Decide to make it your own. Yes, you will think of him cheating every time you pull the red Guernsey over your head and smooth it over your breasts, but a handmade sweater lasts almost forever, more faithful in the end.

Repeat 10 pattern rounds. Begin gussets. At the same time, move out, sell your books, cut your hair, pawn your ring for a little cash that might treat you and a couple of friends to a special dinner and a show. *Continue to work Chart A, until 130 rounds are complete. Begin pattern Chart B.* Quit your job, consign your business clothes, file for divorce, and rent a mountain cabin near a lake you loved as a child.

With wrong side facing, begin back yoke. Learn to use a chainsaw, axe, maul, splitting wedge, and hatchet. They will keep your cottage, which has only a wood stove, warm. Finalize your divorce. Trade the little imported city car bought new primarily because of its easy-to-park size (be honest: for its snob appeal) for a used pickup whose bed—four by four by eight—is the full measure of a cord of wood.

Increase evenly. Reading from right to left, begin pattern Chart C. Adopt ancient neighbor widow's entire litter of seven barn kittens. Notice no more chipmunks, moles, mice, or rats, but your red wool in a frequent tangle. Teach the little cats "no."

Begin front yoke. Read to the blind, pick apples, wait tables, drive a pilot vehicle back and forth and back and forth for the highway department, tutor arithmetic, sew gift shop potholders. Swallow your fear: Put the down payment on the cabin.

Work pattern Charts D, E, and F as set. Begin pattern Charts G and H. Relax at dawn and dusk, knitting the red Guernsey on your porch rocker. In summer, butterflies—blue skippers, orange monarchs, yellow swallowtails—your three white chickens, the country folk along your dirt road, and your neighbor's chestnut mare who longs to get to your apple tree, keep you company. Give the grown kittens to new friends, choosing only the tailless tabby who walks with you every day through the woods to a stream shining with trout.

Using 2 double-pointed or 1 US 2 circular needle, try to begin shoulder strap. Drop stitches, pick them up, get confused, try again, then ask the widow for help. Her hands remember what you want to do even if she can't see that tiny gauge clearly. At the same time, begin driving her to buy groceries, fill prescriptions, and visit her husband's grave.

"I want my ashes spread on my garden," she tells you. "Don't bury my bones in a cold dark hole. Promise?"

Because she has no children either, you promise. Ten months later, you keep your word. When the only distant relative you manage to find expresses no interest in anything next door but the profit from selling the house and the land, adopt her black mutt, chestnut mare, and the surprise buckskin colt who arrives in less than an hour early one frosty autumn morning.

Pick up stitches and work neckband k1p1 for 1 inch. Cast off in rib. Accept the permanent job at the village library. No benefits, no pension, minimum wage. Less in a week than you used to make in a day, but no commute, no dry cleaning, no panty hose, no office politics, no maddening boss. Daily: children with schoolwork, adults with curiosity. You keep finding yourself on the grimy carpet that desperately needs cleaning, books open, saying, "Here. Look. I found something you can use."

With right side facing and US 2 circular needles, pick up stitches from gusset holder, pick up armhole edge, pick up shoulder strap, pick up other armhole edge. Notice the hot flashes, the night sweats, the reading glasses, the morning star, the moon's phases, your land quickening with flowers, year after year.

Work pattern Chart J, shaping sleeve. Gradually understand that the money, the city, the husband, the baby, were not meant for you. *Change to US 1 double-pointed needles. Work cuff in k1p1 rib for 2 inches. Cast off. Repeat for other sleeve.*

Darn in loose ends.

—*Irene Wanner*

"O! grief hath changed me since you saw me last,
And careful hours with time's deformed hand
Have written strange defeatures in my face."

—WILLIAM SHAKESPEARE

a stitch held in eternity

This is wrong. Not acrylic. Natural fibers. Cotton and wool. Those will decay more naturally when exposed to the weather. Not acrylic. I want her little body to be wrapped in something natural. And so on and so on went my thoughts one brisk November day in 1993 as I sat on the edge of my two-year-old daughter's bed ripping out four days' work on her burial blanket. She was asleep next to me, breathing deeply, an activity which took up most of her time in those last few days of her life.

I went to my closet and found a box filled with skeins of natural wool left over from another knitting project, a thick comforter which lay neatly folded on the end of my bed upstairs. Next to the box of wool in the closet was an old metal cylinder filled with my grandmother's knitting needles. Nana taught my mother to knit when she was a young girl, and my mother passed the family tradition on to me. When my grandmother died, I was given all her knitting supplies including the needles I was now using to make Theresa's blanket.

As my daughter rested, I carefully monitored her breathing as I quietly knit one row, purled one row, knit one row, purled one row, over and over and over again. When she woke, I tried to entertain her with toys and books, but she wanted nothing to do with any of it. She was too tired to move. And so as she slept, I sat next to her knitting her blanket and trying to balance my heart on the fine line between knowing she was going to survive and knowing she was going to die. As my fingers kept to their task, my thoughts wandered into a snapshot review of our life together.

Knit one row.

My third child, Theresa, was born with Down Syndrome and congenital heart defects. Though she was at the top of the developmental chart for kids in her category, it took her a long time to learn new things. And while I watched her struggle to breastfeed, crawl, stand, talk, and take her first steps, I learned the art of patience.

My other two children were quick learners; everything came easy to them. As I watched Theresa's learning process broken down into tiny steps, I was given the gift of seeing how normal activities are actually made up of many, many parts, just as a sweater is made up of many, many individual stitches. Watching her learn how to pull herself up in her crib was fascinating. It was like watching slow-motion photography of a blooming rose; I was able to see the beauty of her process.

One day she changed her normal nap routine by moving herself over to the side of the crib, and for the next few days of that new activity, she did nothing more than contemplate her next move. Later on in the week, I watched as her tiny hands grabbed the railing and clenched. I could almost feel her will to do more, but grabbing and clenching was all she could manage for the next several days. Then, little by little, she gained the strength of will and strength of body to pull herself to standing. It took her two full weeks from the first day to the last, but, oh, how she beamed with pride as she looked down over the top railing at the floor before.

"Aanh! Aanh!" she said. And I beamed with pride right back at her. This child worked hard for every accomplishment, and as she slowly developed more and more skills, she was unknowingly teaching me about effort, courage, and will. From my motherly perspective, Theresa was a healthy little girl in spite of having Down Syndrome and heart problems. She didn't suffer from the little maladies like colds and ear infections. And the bigger problems that required attention, like shunt surgery to help her breathe, were addressed when

Karen and Theresa.

necessary. As a family, we learned to be flexible around her physical needs, but when she was diagnosed with leukemia, that flexibility was stretched into learning how to live life half a day at a time.

Purl one row.

One of the physical symptoms of leukemia is excessive bruising. One day I took Theresa to her early intervention pre-school, where I sat in a special parents' room behind a one-way mirror. She was having fun playing with the other children, and I watched with happiness as she climbed up the slide's small three-step ladder with a teacher's aide at her side. Down she slid, laughing joyfully. The aide took her over to the snack table and whispered something to another teacher who then came into the parents' room where I sat.

"Can I talk to you for a minute?" she asked.

"Sure," I said. "What's up? Theresa seems to be having fun today."

"Yes, she does, but I need to talk to you about something else. We've noticed that Theresa has a number of bruises on her face, arms, and legs, and we're required by law to notify the authorities when we see children with a lot of bruises."

My heart sank into the pit of my stomach. Was this woman accusing me of beating my child? I took a deep breath so that I wouldn't burst out in tears. "When I entered Theresa into this school, I told the enrollment people that she has leukemia," I explained. "That's why I always stay here. She needs to be monitored carefully. And she bruises easily. That's why special care has to be taken to make sure she doesn't fall."

Knit one row. Purl one row. Knit one row. Purl one row. The snapshot images of life with Theresa filled my mind.

"Theresa's outgrown her shunt," her heart doctor said.

"Okay. Let's schedule the surgery," I suggested.

"I'm afraid it's not that simple. With her lowered resistance from the leukemia we're concerned that the surgery would put her at risk for infection."

And, I thought, since her heart can't handle the strain of chemotherapy, she's never going to be treated for the leukemia so she's never going to be able to have the shunt surgery.

"What does this mean? I asked.

"It means that as Theresa continues to grow, the shunt she has will become less and less effective."

There was nothing else to say.

Lost in my thoughts about Theresa, I let a few stitches fall off the end of my needle. Carefully, I put them back on and continued to knit. Dropped stitches were a problem I could easily solve. But my daughter's illness was out of my hands. The half-a-day-at-a-time life I'd been living for six months had turned into a minute-by-minute exercise in faith that life has meaning even if I can't understand.

Knit one row.

"The test results show no cancerous cells," the doctor at children's hospital said. We'd gone to seek a second opinion on the leukemia shunt dilemma.

"What do you mean?"

"We ran a series of blood tests and the results show no cancerous cells."

I wanted to argue with him. I wanted to tell him he was wrong. Was he looking at the right tests? Did he have my daughter's chart in front of him? How could this be? No one could offer an explanation. The cancer was gone, and life has meaning even if I can't understand. We enjoyed the summer of Theresa's remission, and by early October, at the age of two years and three months, she'd taken her first steps by herself! I'd never seen her smile so big! But within a few short weeks, her strength began to fail, and I soon realized what the tests would confirm; the leukemia was back. By Halloween she could no longer hold herself up, and by Thanksgiving, though I hoped with every breath that the illness would once again reverse itself, I knew that arrangements had to be made.

Purl one row.

In her last days, Theresa slept for hours, waking up for only a minute or two at a time. I slept with her at night. And during the day I used my grandmother's needles to knit my little girl's burial blanket with leftover yarn from my woolen comforter. The blanket grew in length, but I knew that I would keep knitting until she took her last breath. Knit one row. Purl one row. Each new stitch and each new breath was held in a moment of eternity.

I was blessed with the honor of being Theresa's mother. She taught me patience. She taught me hope, and she taught me that life is a process made up of many, many tiny steps. I learned from Theresa that, no matter how long or how short, no matter how simple or how complex, in the end, every life is whole and complete.

Knit one row. Purl one row. I love you, Theresa.

Karen J. Gordon

"While grief is fresh, every attempt to divert only irritates. You must wait till grief be digested, and then amusement will dissipate the remains of it."

—SAMUEL JOHNSON

inheritance

Mother leaves me her knitting supplies: boxes, baskets, cloth bags, scattered through her apartment. Every size needle. A suitcase full of yarn, never unpacked after she moved here.

We leave her flat intact, spread out into it from the upper floor where we live. We watch her TV, use her towels.

In every closet, woolen afghans, bags of yarn. I give it away and give it away. All the acrylic to churches for charity mittens and hats. Mohair to my friend who makes cloth dolls. A bagful to the handwork teacher at my son's school.

Still I'm left with too much.

Her smell in the fibers of the yarn. In the drawers and cabinets. A strange mix of Korean cooking and mothballs. Garlic and camphorous chemicals.

Inveterate knitter, her hands always moving.

Is this the year I will learn how to knit?

For months I sense her. She never leaves me.

On my birthday, I request knitting lessons from my kids. They've all made scarves, hats, gloves, even socks. My eleven-year-old son teaches me to cast on, up, over, through, pull.

In through the window
Run around the back
Out through the window
Off pops Jack

My hands slip into mother's rhythms. I inherited her short fingers and wrinkly hands instead of father's long elegant ones. I too have busy hands that are rarely still, and a knack for handwork.

A scarf from balls of scrap yarn.

I take her balls of scrap yarn. A thick purple wool, a fine white cotton, a nubby boucle, and a mohair whose fibers always seem to float into my mouth. I knit them all together into one long scarf.

For years every Christmas, new mittens for the kids, with snowflake designs. *Throw them away!* she'd insist if she spotted the old mittens. She promised, *I'll make you new ones every year.*

At one point I find I can no longer knit in public—the scarf is so ugly with its patchwork of odd yarns. The gauge is so uneven that the scarf stretches in and out in width, and my knitting is so sloppy—I never undo. People look askance, feeling sorry for me.

I take her scraps and knit them together. What else have I got?

Her knitting is so fine, too fine. *This will be your inheritance,* she tells me one day, stroking the arm of her white angora sweater with the irises on the back. She bought the pattern at the Boston Museum of Fine Arts. The sweater is so dainty I've never worn it.

I like imperfections. I'm amused by the gauge discrepancies, love using up scraps, and enjoy the bamboo clicking as my knitting becomes easier. I sit in yoga asanas as I knit, opening my hips, deepening my groin, stretching my piriformis in lotus as the scarf lengthens and drapes into my lap.

My children contribute a few rows here and there, grabbing the scarf from me. I begin the bad habit of knitting as I drive, keeping a basket in the passenger seat and doing a few stitches at each red light.

I read a knitting book and wonder, *what is my knitting narrative?* How did these needles end up in my hands? What do I do with them?

Cleaning my mother's bedroom, I find the beginning of something—lavender yarn knit in the round, just the first few rows completed. Her months in the hospital, too sick to knit. Feeding her green Jell-O, half cans of Sprite. Too sick to eat.

Needle Notes

Pilling sweaters? Cut the pills off with a straight razor to restore the sweater's like-new appearance. Is that favorite sweater stretching out? Tighten up cuffs and neck by running a thread of elastic through them.

Every size needle. Skeins and skeins of yarn. Between my mother and my kids I'm set for life. For several months I knit like a fiend—a scarf, a sweater, mittens. I find some red cotton in my daughter's old fourth-grade handwork bag, and think: menstrual pads.

My mother leaves me the wart on her thumb. Are warts hereditary? Under the same fingernail and everything.

Soft, folded red layers in waffle stitch. My son takes a look and says, *You should add flaps and a little button.* So I do. When I knit in restaurants and servers ask me what I'm making, I smile and say, *a washcloth.*

I am unknitting my mother's life. Paying off her medical bills and throwing away her paperwork. Giving away her shoes, selling off her furniture. But which sweaters do I keep, which do I give away? To whom?

For a solid year, I wear her clothes. A scarf, a sweater, a sports bra, whatever, each day. Finally I stop, tired of her things.

Going through the knitting book, I try out all the stitches in my "washcloths" until I run out of red yarn.

She moves on. I can feel it, can smell it. In the first year I didn't miss her. I wore her, carried her, immanent. But now—

Someone else moves into her flat. Moving my stuff back upstairs, I find another knitting project in a closet. The beginning of a sock my daughter started and forgot about, in a tangle of thick wool. I pick it up, knitting and purling to continue the ribbing.

But now—

It's summer and I haven't knit in months. Tomorrow we leave for vacation, driving to the East Coast. I bring the unfinished sock and the tangled wool.

Peggy Hong

mother

Just don't forget, call me when you arrive,
she always said. Or write. At least do that.
On all my trips abroad, I did contrive
to find a phone and then relieved I sat,
free for the moment, trying to combat
the shackles of her love. Yet now in anguish,
to feel them tight on me is what I wish.

I walk into what was my mother's room,
at present used by guests as well as me.
I'm safe in it as though it were her womb.
Around myself I wrap a shawl that she
crocheted and as I look about I see
designs she made for scarves in lacy bands.
I finger them and touch my mother's hands.

It is ten years already since she died.
Some days go by when I don't think of her.
Maybe they're easy, still I know that I'd
in spite of it much rather feel the burr
against my heart and strain to hear the stir
of voice so gentle it all harm allays.
I beg of you, don't give me easy days.

≈Elisa Merkl

dropped stitches

I have knit since I was a small child at my grandmother's side, sitting on a stool next to her rocking chair. I remember the steel needles and the ball of red yarn vividly, the few stitches on the needles and the concentration it took to do it right, just like she was doing. She coached me along for a number of years. The first pair of mittens she helped me knit were pink; I was about nine years old. Grandmothers of that time period did not use patterns; she just told me what to do and when to do it. Everything went smoothly, but my mittens, when they were done, were a little off: one had a pointed tip, the other, a rounded tip. This was all part of the experience of knitting. My grandmother became ill and had to go to a nursing home, but the grandmotherly lady across the street took over where my grandmother had left off and I kept right on knitting. I made a number of sweaters through my high school years as the lady across the street taught me to read patterns.

Since that time, I have always turned to knitting for peace. I have made time every day to do some knitting, leaving the daily duties of housework and keeping a family undone if necessary. That is, I did until four and a half years ago, when my husband died of cancer. It was a short illness and then he was gone, and along with him, the comfort of knitting left me. I could not knit. I would pick up my knitting and put it down. My therapist suggested a schedule of knitting one minute at a time and then putting it down until the next day. And then, after a while, two minutes a day, and then three and so on until I could sit in the chair for ten minutes and knit.

I would set the timer and do this. Sometimes it was very diffi- cult for me. I did it and can say that I am now back to knitting. Not full-time, but I am being productive in my process of healing with my knitting and have many pairs of socks for Christmas next year. I have progressed to making a vest for myself and am halfway done. I guess you could say I'm getting back into the swing of things. I am not really sure what caused me to stop when my husband died, but a lot stopped in my life when he died. It was odd to me that I felt I could no longer knit, as knitting had always been with me through everything. I'm grateful for my therapist's suggestion.

There is always someone out there to help you learn something new, and there's always someone new to teach the knitting to— that's what makes the world go around, doesn't it?

Catherine Davis

"One sought not absolute truth. One sought only a spool on which to wind the thread of history without breaking it."

—HENRY BROOKS ADAMS

Easy Shawl

Knit a simple shawl to keep you warm in your season of grief. With size 11 needles and a worsted-weight yarn, cast on three stitches. Knit every row, increasing one stitch at the beginning of each and every row. The shawl will grow into a triangle shape. When it looks just the right size to wrap yourself in, cast off.

Needle Notes

Choose your needles to work well with the yarn you are using. For instance, if you're working with a fuzzy kind of yarn, metal needles are a good choice. Metal are also recommended if speed is important to you; the stitches will slip off the needles effortlessly. If you're knitting with slippery yarns, though, like a mercerized cotton, linen, or silk, you'll want a needle that's not so slippery, lest you lose those precious stitches. Try bamboo or wood. My favorite needles are made of ebony. They feel like a treasure in the hands; paired with cashmere, ebony needles make for the ultimate knitting experience.

Nine: Knitting Up Warmth

"In the winter, warmth stands for all virtue."

—HENRY DAVID THOREAU

One of the greatest benefits of knitting is that it allows us to clothe ourselves and our loved ones in beautiful handmade works of art and to create our own nurturing warmth. This is an especially valuable skill on days when the world seems a cold and harsh place. Knitting connects generations together, links up friends in new ways, reminds us of the bounty of the earth and of our unique ability to use that bounty to bless those around us. Knowing how to knit is a great gift we have received from others, and which we may, in turn, offer as a heartfelt legacy to our children, the people we work with, our extended family, our community. Whether we gift those in our lives with finished items, or pass on our knowledge of the craft itself, our knitting cannot help but enrich the lives of those around us.

In BJ Nathan Hegedus's "Tales of an Afghan," we see how a grandmother's presence is made manifest in an afghan she knit before her premature death—a heartfelt reminder of her life to a granddaughter who didn't know her. Leslie Petrovski's "Pass It On" recounts a mother-daughter connection strengthened with knitting. Novelist Michelle Huneven celebrates an orphan sweater that found a home with her, and poet David Starkey explores how romantic love knits itself into the fabric of our lives.

If you've never taught someone to knit, ask around. If you'd like to know more about knitting, don't be shy—see if there's someone nearby who might be hungry to pass on his or her know-how and love of the craft. Share the abundance you've received and rejoice in the gifts of your hands.

"Washing a real sweater is akin to bathing a baby, and brings the same satisfaction of producing a clean, pretty, sweet-smelling creature."
—ELIZABETH ZIMMERMAN, *Knitting Without Tears*

tales of an afghan

I never felt the circling of her arms around me as I nestled in her lap. I never breathed the scent of her perfume; I don't even know what she wore. I never heard the sound of her voice; was it earthy and deep or light and gay? But I did get to know her and know of her, and that was through the afghan.

My grandmother died seven years before I was born, at the age of forty-two. A heavy antique gold link bracelet, some black-and-white photographs, several Christmas ornaments, and a simple patterned afghan were the few items of hers that my mother possessed. The bracelet was kept in my mother's dresser drawer. The jagged-edged pictures, fragile by the passage of time, had been placed in an album using black triangle corners with glue on the back. The delicate mercury glass ornaments sat most of the year packed in a trunk in the basement of our apartment building.

The afghan lay on the arm of the living room couch, an everyday inanimate object in the midst of our young vivacious family's life.

Multicolored squares 6 inches in length were whipstitched

together. There was no apparent pattern to the placement of colors, and only a few colors were repeated, though the afghan was large enough to cover a twin bed. The squares were all garter-stitched using number five needles. Every square was perfect. Row after row of stitches were uniform, the yarn tension consistent. Each square an exact replica of the ones surrounding it, perfect 90-degree angles, precise in length. Framing the knitted squares was a band of orange, an inch of single crochet stitches. A scalloped crochet border of green single stitches bound it all together.

My grandmother's afghan was flawless, fastidiously crafted. There was no bunching or buckling along the seams. No stitchery stretched to match an unmatched mate. It laid flat and straight, a smooth cover of many colors. The contrast of basic patterns with mastery skill was a study in dignity and grace.

Edna Volcek was the third-youngest of nine children. Her parents—my great-grandparents—had come to America from Czechoslovakia, part of the wave of Europeans seeking a better life. The Volceks became the Vlecks, as it was the fashion to shorten names. Soon after the death of her mother, Edna contracted scarlet fever. Without antibiotics, this worsened into rheumatic fever, damaging my grandmother's heart. Though she recovered, her health was to remain frail.

My grandfather Paul, having recently emigrated from Germany after World War I, first saw my grandmother from across a street. She sat in the window of a barbershop, giving a manicure. He crossed the road and walked into the shop to have his nails done. Smitten with her pretty face, big eyes, flapper dress, and modern bobbed hair, he wooed her and they were married. My mother, Gloria, was born a year later; Edna was just twenty-one. The pregnancy had taken its toll, and my mother would remain an only child.

Edna loved to cook and she loved to knit and crochet. Tiring easily, without the stamina for much physical activity, knitting became a passion, and her skill proficient. My mother's wardrobe was filled with woolen treasures.

We would sit on the couch, my sister Stacey and I, and ask our mother questions about the grandmother we had never known. She would reach for the afghan and point to the different squares of color. "This grey was a sweater coat and matching hat, this navy a pleated skirt. And this"—as she pointed to a square of plum, laughing—"was a disastrous bathing suit." Each square a memory, a recollection of an outfit, of a day, a time, an era.

"It was the Depression," our mother told us. "Nothing was ever wasted; we watched every penny. My allowance for the week was ten cents; I could go to the movies for that. Your grandmother would use leftover yarn to make squares for afghans. She made many blankets, giving them away as gifts over the years."

I ran my small hand over the squares of color, touching the yarn that Edna had touched, hearing the rhythmic clicking of

The author learns to knit.

needles, her hands a blur of movement. The patches were a conduit through the years to what had been. I imagined my mother as a girl, dressed in the sweaters and hats and skirts that were described to me as we sat on the couch, the three of us. These memories were all that I had from which to craft the grandmother that I had never known.

Pointing to a kelly green square one evening, as we nestled together, our mother told Stacey and me the story of the green shoes and the electric bill. It seems that the power was due to be turned off unless the account was settled up. Edna set out to pay the debt in person. As she walked toward the power company building she passed a shoe store. In the window was a pair of kelly green shoes, a perfect match for an outfit she had just finished making. That night, when our grandfather got home from work, he was greeted by a house bathed in warm candlelight. "Isn't it romantic?" my grandmother smiled as she reached up to hug him, wearing her green dress and new shoes.

Our mother's stories told of rolling cigarettes at the kitchen table—my grandmother smoked Old Gold. Rides with her cousins to Jones Beach sitting in the rumble seat of my grandfather's Model T Ford, a picnic basket filled with deviled egg sandwiches, a Mason jar of Tom Collins discreetly tucked in the corner for the adults.

There were tales of our grandmother purposely switching checks for bills due so that they would be sent back, mistake noted, apology given, thus buying an extra few days in which to make the payments. When our extremely skinny mother and her thin cousin moaned about being teased and called "six o'clock" our grandmother retorted, "The meat closest to the bone is the best!"

The laughter, the smell of apple turnovers, the sounds of jazz, the twinkling of her eyes, her wit, her full-of-fun, devil-may-care cheeky approach to life—these are the stories the afghan gave forth.

Stacey and I had no grandparents. Our paternal grandmother and grandfather had died when we were young. The stories our mother told us about her life as a girl were our link to a grandmother we had never met. The afghan wove our lives together, giving her presence, as if she was sitting with us on the couch.

"What did grandma die of?" I asked one night as we sat together, the afghan tucked around us.

"Grandma's heart was growing weaker and weaker. Her body was starting to shut down. She died of kidney failure," Mom answered.

"Did it hurt?"

"No, she just slowly slipped away."

As Edna was slipping away, the war was on. It was a time of Victory gardens, rationing, and doing without. Due to a shortage of nylon, my mother and her cousins learned to draw straight lines down the backs of their legs using eyebrow pencils, creating the illusion of wearing seamed stockings. Mom had auditioned and been given a spot in a U.S.O. tour leaving for Europe. She had a soprano voice and was thrilled to be given the opportunity to be with professional performers.

Edna's health was starting to rapidly fail. My mother turned down the U.S.O. tour to stay at home and take care of her. She told us how she painted the dining room in their house apple green, Edna's favorite color. Her mother, no longer able to climb the stairs, now slept in that room. My mother nursed her mother that last year. She cooked, cleaned, and did laundry. My grandmother died quietly at home, my mother and grandfather at her side.

"Did you cry when your mother died?" I asked.

"Yes, I was very sad, but she had been sick for such a long time, it was not a shock when it happened," she replied. I remember grappling with the magnitude of emotion I felt at the thought of my own mother dying. It was unimaginable to think of life without her, yet she seemed so calm as she talked about her mother's passing away, she didn't get teary-eyed or anything. It must be that she had been twenty-one and all grown up when it happened, I reasoned.

"Do you miss her?"

"I think about her often." She hugged me and said, "You know, grandma is with me, here in my heart forever."

My first knitting endeavor was executed on thick wooden needles with red balls on the ends. The orange yarn was a mess of dropped stitches and mysteriously picked-up ones. Casting on had been a painful process, with the yarn tension so tight I could barely get my needle in to make a stitch. My mother was no help; she had inherited her mother's love of cooking but replaced her needlecraft with a love of sewing. I quickly gained new respect for the afghan draped on the arm of the couch.

With the aid of a neighbor, my stitches slowly became even and neat. "Practice makes perfect," my mother would offer. Having mastered casting on and a simple garter stitch, I managed a basic scarf, our neighbor binding off the last row for me. Though a little wavy and curled, it was a noble start.

A comforting afghan for a day home sick from school.

In time I learned to knit and crochet many things. I especially loved to make baby sweaters patterned with ducks or sailboats using brightly colored yarn—one-of-a-kind gifts celebrating new life. We brought our daughter home from the hospital, all 5 pounds 15 ounces of her, swathed in a hooded white crocheted sweater with small pastel buttons.

The years passed, and the afghan was in constant need of repair. My mother would darn and reattach squares as needed. Besides filling our hearts and heads with memories, it covered my sister and me as we watched TV, as we lay on the couch sick with strep throat waiting for Dr. Weber. Its colorful memories enveloped us as we fell asleep waiting for our dad to return from a business trip.

Finally, there was nothing left to darn. Time, moths, use, life claimed the tattered afghan. I don't know what my mother did with it, but one day it was gone. She was not one for saving things and must have tossed it out. What went through her mind as she gathered it up? Her childhood and ours recorded in this shabby woolen remnant. "Oh, the stories it could tell, if only it could speak," she laughingly said throughout the years.

Six months after Edna died, my grandfather asked my mother to find an apartment. He was remarrying and needed the space. He helped my mother move into a studio apartment in the Village.

My mother's marriage to my father was a small affair. They were married in the rabbi's study with his family present. There had been a momentary crisis when my mother refused to sign a paper saying she would raise the children to be Jewish. She claimed to be agnostic and not a believer in organized religion. This view had sprung from an incident as a small girl in Sunday school. She had been asked to leave for being too inquiring.

My grandfather was not present. It was unacceptable to him that his daughter was marrying a Jew. He never had anything to do with her or us the rest of his life. We wondered about our grandfather. But you cannot miss what you have never known. Our mother would shake her head and laugh, "Wait until he dies and Grandma gets her hands on him." She never dwelt on being abandoned, though it surely crushed her heart.

When my sister married her first husband, my mother sent her father an announcement with a simply written note: "Imagine all that you've missed . . ." My grandfather died a year before my daughter—his first great-grandchild—was born. Our entire childhood, he lived less than half an hour away from my sister and me and never came to see us. I have never understood how my wonderful grandmother could have loved him.

As I have now passed the age at which my grandmother died, I realize how tragically young she was. Stacey and I nursed our mother as she lost her fight with cancer. She burst into tears one day and sobbed that she had never wanted her daughters to do what she had done. Yet that is what daughters do, they stand resilient, though their hearts are breaking, and fight to make every moment the most comfortable that it can be. They cry tears in hot steamy showers, the water drowning out anguished sobs. And they do this day after day.

My daughter, Jenevieve, was able to get to know her grandmother "Gigi" before she died; for this gift I am truly grateful. She is the only girl of five grandchildren and the only one who has her own memories of her grandmother to recall. Her then four-year-old eyes took in and saved the times they spent together, crystal-clear recollections, enhancing the stories that my sister and I tell. And we tell lots of stories, so that all our children will know these women. We savor and cherish our tales, perhaps because the abruptness with which they end makes what we call to mind so precious.

Jenevieve is now twenty. I listen to her sing, her beautiful mezzo-soprano voice filling the room with passion and dreams, and I hear my mother. My sister and I cook "Cinderella" cakes from a recipe in our mother's childhood cookbook, the smell of baking vanilla filling the air. My needles click together softly, making beanies for my children to pull down low on their heads. Four generations of women, the threads that bind us together like the whipstitched patches of a simple knitted afghan.

BJ Nathan Hegedus

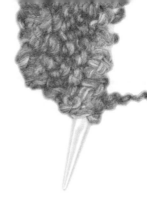

pass it on

🕉 Women of my generation—I am forty-three—received spotty instruction in housekeeping, as if our mothers were unsure about how to prepare us for a postfeminist world. My mother took a middle road, insisting I learn to cook, because everybody has to eat, and to knit, because she understood how nourishing this skill could be too.

We started with some scraps left from a sweater my mother made for my grandmother—a pale gold cable knit with pewter buttons—and a pair of aluminum Boye needles. I was no more than eight years old. She cast on a few stitches and we decided I would make a scarf. The needles felt unwieldy at first and splayed out from my small hands like oars. Each stitch seemed a mystery, a tangled string-game, Cat's Cradle with sticks. For a child, or any beginner, there is no logic in the loopy ladders formed by the yarn; rather one attacks each stitch as it comes until the muscles remember on their own.

I knit aggressively at first, stabbing my right needle into the breach between fiber and metal, then lashing it vigorously with my working yarn. Pulling too hard as I knit, I found my stitches clinging to the colored metal stubbornly, refusing to march toward the nib of my needle. Impatient, I would yank with my right arm, slipping everything off the left needle.

"Mom!" I would yell.

"Rip it out!"

Then she cast on again. And again. Furiously, I jabbed at my work, dropping stitches and increasing by accident. I knit with the tail and split stitches.

"OK, now watch . . ." she said. Knit, knit, knit. Her garter stitches lined up like rows of new peas.

"I can't!"

"Remember *The Little Engine That Could?*" she asked. By the age of eight, I was well acquainted with the story of the smug little steam engine that chugged its way to the top of the mountain. *The Little Engine That Could* was my mother's metaphor of last resort. Yet even images of that determined locomotive couldn't clarify the mechanics of this baffling art in my eight-year-old mind.

Frustrated, I eventually threw my project into the hall closet, where it sat for a year or two before I attempted again.

I'm not sure what compelled me to drag that horrible scrap of knitting from the closet shelf, except that ours was a creative household and a knotted mass of yarn held more appeal than the boredom of a long summer or a stuffy winter break. I dug it out of the bag, newly interested, and my mother shaped my small fingers around the needles, again showing me the awkward technique. This time it made sense. The stitches contained inherent rhythm, in-around-under-off, in-around-under-off. I clicked happily away. My headscarf grew, misshapen and full of holes, but it grew nonetheless. My mother showed me how to bind off—so easy!—and we tied two pieces of yarn to each side to hold the scarf in place.

I wore that hideous butter-colored headband like a tiara.

Once I got the hang of it, we planned more elaborate projects. Mom encouraged me to make my own choices, like the hot pink and aqua scarf I knit for my Barbie and the wretched stocking cap in burgundy and lilac that hung down to my butt—with sweater to match. Young love prompted a lesson in intarsia; we designed a ski hat that said "Beethoven" on one side, "Einstein" on the other— this for my first boyfriend in junior high. From a magazine, I knit "Farrah's Sweater." This was back in those days when mainstream women's magazines featured knitting patterns, as it was assumed that most women knitted. I had hoped I would look as blow-dried and tan as Ms. Fawcett, the tunic slouched over one bronze shoulder, but I ended up giving the sweater away, hating its clumsy bulk. From then on, I always had a project going even if it languished for months awaiting the run of a high-school play, college finals, or the busy early weeks of a new romance. (A breakup required *lots* of knitting.)

When my grandfather lay dying, my mother knit obsessively, filling a closet with yarn stashed against her grief. Knitting would also see me through the most difficult period of my life, when my thyroid, the small bow-tie-shaped gland regulating so many of our metabolic processes, went haywire and I became so anxious I could barely live in my own skin. With my hormones in an uneasy froth, I wasn't sure how to manage the anger and fear that spilled out of me. Although I hadn't reached for my knitting bag in a couple of years, I pulled it down from the hall closet and discarded a stalled project. After a trip to the yarn store netted a bag of glossy Egyptian cotton, I was on my way.

By focusing on the aqua and yellow overalls for my dear friend's baby or the chenille afghan for the couch—by getting outside myself—I stitched away the evenings until they became something to enjoy rather than endure. The fabric spooled out from my needles in lovely, satisfying swatches, the process of creation, of generation, healing in subtle ways. It is not exaggeration to say that my creative work and the ministrations of my loving family saved me.

In recent years, my mother and I have become knitting evangelists of sorts. This holiday season, we taught my husband's twenty-three-year-old cousin to knit; she just completed an afghan for her first apartment. At an arts festival, I shoved needles and a skein of multicolored yarn at one of my best friends, who has since become so enamored of the craft that she's contemplating a career change. I bought needles and yarn for another friend, who has complained for years about her boring life. "If you're knitting," I told her, "your life can't be boring." Now she's pregnant and planning her first knit layette.

This fall I'll teach my first class at our local yarn store. Though I am no master knitter, I have certain strengths—a way with color and a propensity to finish the projects I begin—which I hope to translate into a class on creative holiday gifts to make . . . and complete. I look forward to the girly camaraderie that accompanies the creation of a fun handbag or faux-fur scarf. And I hope my students come away with a new way of seeing common objects in their world—a knitted lipstick case? A felted jewelry roll? Why not?

But this I know for sure: From the ripping and fixing and demonstrating I've done so far—where the architecture of stitches and garments have revealed themselves—I will learn far more than they. George Bernard Shaw put it beautifully when he wrote, "I'm not a teacher: Only a fellow-traveler of whom you asked the way. I pointed ahead—ahead of myself as well as you."

My mother teaches knitting too. And she is a favorite with students. This passing on of craft delights her, because she believes creative projects can sustain and connect women even during the toughest times. "I'm so glad you knit," she said a few months ago, when I visited for finishing help on a sweater. "Handwork dies if young people don't carry it on."

Though I'm the one who shared my mother's passed-down knowledge with my friends—my generation—they drive the distance to my mother's house in suburban Denver for help when they run into snags with their work. My mother, secretly pleased, unravels their mistakes and shares this bit of wisdom, something I heard from her over and over as I was learning: "First you learn to see your mistakes, and then you learn to fix them." When I asked my pregnant friend why she didn't ask *me* for help, she explained, "Because she knows more than you do." And, "*She's* nicer."

My mother taught herself to knit by deciphering drawings from a how-to book in the 1940s. I learned curled up next to her, her arms around me to demonstrate the stitches. We never forget the people who give us the things that see us through. How lovely for me and this family of friends that we learned from her. How lovely that we will always remember that.

Leslie Petrovski

POODLE PULLOVER
by LESLIE PETROVSKI, WITH ASSISTANCE FROM
KNITWARE SWEATER DESIGN SOFTWARE 2.30

This is a waist-length pullover with bracelet-length sleeves and loop-stitch trim.

FINISHED MEASUREMENTS:
Chest: 40"
Body length (without collar): 20"
Sleeve length: 12" (from armpit, not including cuff)

MATERIALS:
Bulky-weight yarn: 1,400 yards, used double-stranded for body
Worsted-weight yarn: 100 yards, used triple-stranded for loop stitch collar and cuffs
(I used Brown Sheep Company Lamb's Pride Bulky and Worsted in Onyx and Crème.)
One pair size 17 US needles
One pair size 19 US needles

GAUGE: in stocking stitch 1.75 sts = 1 inch, 2.75 rows = 1 inch

PATTERN STITCHES:
Loop stitch:
Row 1: Knit.
Row 2: Insert the needle knitwise and knit one stitch without pulling it off the left-hand needle. Bring the yarn in front as if to purl and

wrap it around your left thumb (this forms the loop). Then knit into the same stitch still remaining on your left-hand needle and slip off. You now have two stitches on your right needle. Pass the first stitch over the second. Repeat across the row.

Row 3: Repeat Rows 1 and 2.

BACK:

1. Cast on 37 stitches using two strands bulky-weight yarn on size 19 needles. Work a garter-stitch hem for 2 inches.

2. Change to stocking stitch. Work even until piece measures 9 ins, excluding hem.

3. **ARMHOLE SHAPING:** Cast off 1 stitches at beginning of next 2 rows.

   Raglan shaping: (WS rows: P2, P2tog, purl across row until you reach the last 4 stitches, P2Tbl, P2.)

   (RS rows: K2, SSK, knit across row until you reach the last 4 stitches, K2tog, K2.)

4. Use your raglan shaping every 3rd row 4 times, then every 2nd row 6 times.

   (I like right- and left-slanting decreases on raglans, but you can simplify the pattern by replacing the SSK and P2Tbl with plain old K2tog and P2tog respectively.)

5. Place remaining 15 stitches on holder for back of neck.

FRONT:

1.–2. Follow steps 1 and 2 as for back.
3. **ARMHOLE:** Dec for armholes as for back. Continue until armhole measures 6½ inches, with 23 stitches remaining. Then shape neckline as follows, continuing raglan shaping at the same time.
4. **SHAPE NECK:** Work both sides at the same time. Work 9 stitches. Slip the next 5 sts to a holder. With a second ball of yarn, work remaining 9 stitches. Continue armhole shaping. Dec 1 stitch at neck edge every row 3 times.
5. Work even at neck edge, continuing armhole decreases to last 2 stitches. Cast off.

SLEEVES:

1. Cast on 18 stitches on size 17 needles using triple-stranded worsted-weight yarn. Work in loop stitch for 2 inches (two pattern repeats) in worsted-weight yarn.
2. Change to main color yarn, size 19 needles, and stocking stitch.
3. Inc 1 stitch at each end of every 6th row twice, then every 7th row twice to 26 stitches.
4. Work even until sleeve measures 11 inches, excluding hem.
5. **SHAPE CAP:** Cast off 1 stitch at beg of next two rows. Dec 1 stitch at each end of every 2nd row 12 times until no stitches remain.

LEFT SHOULDER SEAM:

1. Sew left sleeve to front and back, and right sleeve to front only, along raglan armhole seams.

LOOP STITCH FUNNEL NECK:
Use size 17 needles and triple-stranded worsted-weight yarn.

1. With right side of work facing, pick up and knit 15 stitches from back neck holder, 5 stitches from left front neck edge, 5 stitches from front neck holder, and 5 stitches from right front neck edge. Total 30 stitches.
2. Row 1 knit across, dec 6 stitches evenly across row. Continue, beginning with Row 2 of the loop stitch pattern for 2 inches (a total of two pattern repeats).
3. Cast off very loosely using Row 2 of the loop stitch pattern.

Finishing: Sew remaining shoulder seam. Check that the collar will stretch to fit over the head.

FINISHING:
1. Sew sleeve top to armhole, easing to fit. Sew side and sleeve seams using invisible seam. Sew any remaining seams.
2. Weave in all loose ends.
3. Block if necessary.

flame stitch

O love, how you have woven yourself

into my life, what patterns you've led
me to follow—reversible at times

with a ragged border. Long needle

that never works even. Knit and purl,
knit and purl: you're smooth

on one side, bumpy on the other.

Ivory, dark sage, raspberry—
the colors you show me

pulse as I study you in lamplight.

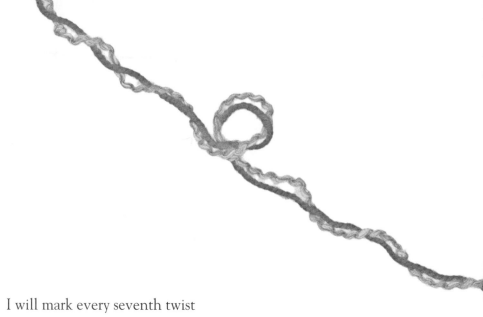

I will mark every seventh twist
in our affair by tying a tag

of scrap yarn through the crossover.

When we are finished, I will bind off
the end loosely, leaving enough room

for the inevitable stretching of memory.

David Starkey

the orphan sweater

I am doing a quarterly task, folding the sweaters and shawls in my cedar chest. I learned from a shop owner how to fold them so that they look as perfect and wear as neatly as a sweater fresh from the store shelf. But a chest is just a box, and I am given, usually at those times when I should have been long dressed and out the door, to occasional desperate rummaging. After so much frantic digging, my expertly folded sweaters have sprawled, tangling arms like so many languorous lovers. When I start pulling out sweaters with unwanted ruchings and the rivery creases of 3-D topographical maps, I know it's time to set things in order. I do not mind this every-few-months task of folding. I have more than a passing feeling for my sweaters; I am, in fact, a sweater lover, sweater collector, even a sweater obsessive. David Byrne once sang that his life could be measured out in shirts; with my life, it's sweaters and the occasional shawl and muffler.

I've heard that people, when shopping, tend to buy the same thing over and over again—some people buy belts or jackets; Byrne clearly bought shirts; and with me, yes, it's sweaters, ideally cashmere sweaters, though cotton cardigans and fine merino wool have also won my heart. Sweaters are small, portable, easy to carry off without feeling as if one has made a major purchase—the ideal impulse buy.

But it's also more than that. In general, I like most knitted things far more than their woven counterparts. Between a blazer and a cardigan, I'll always choose the latter; between a jacket and a shawl, no contest. I'll reach for a knitted lap robe before any blanket. It's the give of knit things, the flexibility, the way they move when I move, and the cozy, breathing quality of their warmth. Sweaters mold to the body; they are adaptable, responsive, *willing*.

My own sweaters assume that much, and more, for I have worn them and they carry with them traces of my life; it is as if they are knit first with yarn, then knit again, by use, into the particulars of my own experience. My favorite sweaters have history; some tell stories.

✂✂✂✂

The cedar chest itself came to me eight or nine years ago, after a bad infestation of moths had wreaked serious damage in my closet—and raised my consciousness about mothproofing. Uncharacteristically, my father asked what I wanted for my birthday that year. (This was, I believe, the first and only time he hadn't simply presented me with a check.) "A cedar chest," I said, and not long afterwards he drove up to my house with this sturdy, handsome antique.

Just as Walter Benjamin suggests the most praiseworthy way to fill a library is to write the books yourself, the most praiseworthy way to fill a cedar chest clearly is to knit the woolens yourself. But there is a lamentable absence of ability in my hands, and the chest is filled with sweaters made by others' hands.

Here, let's take a look. Maybe we'll find something you might like to borrow. Or perhaps there's something I'm tired of, and want to give away. Or maybe there's something of interest here—oh, the cashmeres are always of interest to me, intrinsically—a deep weakness, I'll admit. I still don't have nearly enough. Every year, there's a color I want, a color I think I can't live without. This year, it's burgundy or marrow or oxblood. Last year, brown. And see these reds? That was three years ago. I bought one, then found a better one. Two reds. Oh, but I can't quite part with either one.

Here is a gray-and-white thick hand-knitted cashmere funnel neck. I bought it at a cashmere store on impulse and it was very expensive, and I don't regret it.

Here is a burnt orange cardigan. I bought it on sale or I never would've settled for that particular color, which I have come to love. I wore it as my house sweater for at least a year—the one I pulled on before the fire warmed the room, or when the warmth didn't reach my study, or when I slipped outside to the mailbox, or went in the garden to pick lettuce. See, the elbows are wearing thin. It's on the wear-rarely list now, because I love it and I want it to last.

Here is a navy cardigan—I wanted a black one, but they didn't have one in my size. Another one I learned to love and that did common household duty until, on reassessment, I decided it was too good for that.

Here is the delicate brown cardigan I bought last year. The neck is nicely worked, crewed, but subtly squared off; it's a seriously good sweater, too good for my rough use—I huddle with my knees against my chest, welcome my terrier into my arms; I sometimes haul logs in from out of doors, even in my good clothes. Already this one's pilling. I wore it constantly with a brown cashmere skirt also knit, an ensemble of rich blurry brown and mink-like softness, all easy warmth and accommodation—though there's already a small hole in the skirt (the terrier's paw).

Down toward the bottom are the mistakes. A raspberry-pink, shoulder-baring lightweight wool boucle—hey, I just wanted to buy something, okay? Oh, and here's that taupe Dries Van Noten, bought at a ludicrously high full price after numerous visits. Once, when I came to try it on a third or fourth time, it had been sold, which made me want it even more. When it came back to the store—having not worked out with the buyer's wardrobe—I irrationally and incorrectly took it as a sign that this taupe wonder was meant for me, whereas I should have considered how it would serve *my* wardrobe. As an odd, highly stylized piece, with a short cut and extra long arms of peculiarly heavy wool, it's actually more *objet* than wearable item and indeed, I've worn it only a handful of times. If that.

※※※

But here, way at the bottom, are two objects that I no longer wear but cannot bear to throw out. This navy blue pullover with the floppy collar was my first cashmere sweater. There are holes in the armpits and elbows, it's really quite useless. I think that someday I'll make a little pillow out of it. Something soft for my cheek. I love this sweater. It was not one, however, that I bought. Nor was it a gift. If I were perfectly honest, I'd have to say that I stole it.

I found the navy blue sweater around twenty years ago when I worked in the restaurant of a private country club. It showed up in the lost and found, which was a shelf and a couple of cardboard boxes in the closet where the pieces of the dance floor were stored and coats were checked during banquets and dinner dances in the cold months of the year. I noticed the sweater the moment I touched it while rummaging for someone's lost Ray-Bans—that characteristic cashmere softness, the way the yarn itself slows your fingers, makes itself known. This was in May, when the mornings were cool but the days could become quite warm, just the kind of weather when lightweight sweaters are left behind in golf carts or forgotten on chair backs in restaurants. The sweater remained in the lost and found box all summer. I know. I kept my eye on it. Every month, the club newsletter reminded members to claim their lost items, and the boxes saw a halting flow of solo fingerless golf gloves, sunglasses, the occasional Members Only windbreaker or soiled visor, half-used score pads, the stray hand-knit wood-club covers.

One day, around mid-November, when we banquet waitresses were gearing up for a busy party season, my boss took me into the closet to clean it out for the deluge of coats and jackets and umbrellas to come. We went through the lost and found, tossing the unclaimed Members-Only jacket, a bald baby doll with her perforated head, a polyester scarf, some

Needle Notes

What is cashmere? One of the most wonderful fibers one could ever knit or wear (lightweight warmth that's downright sensual next to bare skin), cashmere comes from the undercoat of the underbelly of a goat (any kind of goat) that's exposed to harsh conditions. Not an inexpensive option, but the most aesthetically pleasing yarn I've ever used. Just knitting it feels like ultimate luxury.

papers and tees and sweatbands. I held up the navy blue sweater. "This has been here forever," I said.

"I know," she said, and touched the knit. "I'm surprised nobody's claimed it."

I pulled it over my head. I didn't care how it looked. It felt like a tangible form of affection. "Can I take it?"

"Sure," she said. "But don't wear it around work, just in case."

I wore it everywhere else, at home, to town, to holiday parties. Although a size large, it draped sweetly on my then scrawny frame. As the autumn chill deepened, I grabbed it first thing in the morning, first thing in the night when I changed out of my work clothes. This was the sweater that inducted me into the heaven of cashmere, introduced me to its lightweight snugness, its uncanny ability to keep me perfectly warm within a wide range of temperature. Some years later, long after I quit working at the country club, I would see that same sweater in an assortment of colors on a table in Bergdorf Goodman's in New York City, and witness with a shock that they cost as much as a large household appliance. Later still, when I became a restaurant reviewer and published a novel, I would be able to afford to buy such a sweater every now and then. But back when I worked banquets at the country club, when the only way I could obtain a cashmere pullover was to lift it from a lost and found, I was actually oblivious to the sweater's monetary value and utterly enthralled by its deep night-blue hue and lightly given warmth, its compelling, generous softness.

One night, playing fiddle with a friend's band at a roadhouse forty miles from home, I took off the sweater and forgot to take it home. I called as soon as I realized the lapse, and I was there the next morning when the place opened at eleven. I couldn't bear to be without it. I wouldn't let it sit in any lost and found.

About a month later, in the middle of December, when we banquet waitresses were serving large holiday parties every night, my boss called me into her office just as I showed up for work. "Michelle," she said, "I found out who owns the navy blue sweater."

She then mentioned the name of a member whom I liked, a woman whose last name was a household word thanks to a household product manufactured by her father. "She said she left it here last spring, and has been meaning to ask about it."

"Oh," I said. It hardly seemed fair that a woman who didn't care about this sweater for six months could suddenly lay greater claim to it than I, who adored it, who drove eighty miles to retrieve it within twelve hours the time I left it somewhere. Then again, it was her sweater, and my boss knew it. "Okay," I said. "I'll bring it in."

My boss frowned slightly. She was about ten years older than I was, and strict in a reasonable, trustworthy way. I'd worked for her for three years by then and considered her a friend. I also respected her—and depended on her—as my employer. I knew her to be thoughtful and fair and stern only when she needed to be. "I told her I'd look for it," she said. "I didn't say I'd seen it."

"I'll bring it tomorrow," I said miserably.

"Why don't you talk to the other girls about it," my boss said. "See what they have to say, and then get back to me."

This seemed to me an odd way of going about things, but I assumed there were nuances or issues at stake to which I was oblivious. So I went into the break room, where the other five waitresses were assembling for the night's work. From working together very hard—as banquet waitresses, we tended to work ten- and twelve-hour shifts and did lots of heavy lifting (arranging tables, assembling the portable but heavy dance floor)—we had become fierce friends with each other. It was a unique, tough kind of allegiance I haven't enjoyed since. I brought up the matter of the sweater. "She left the sweater in the lost and found for six months," I said. "But it's hers, and I should give it back . . . right?"

One waitress—the one with the most seniority—shook her head. "It's too suspicious. First C— (our boss) couldn't produce it, and then she could. The members here are already convinced we steal from them. They'll just automatically think that again. I say you don't give it back."

"It's not like you stole it," said another waitress. "You cleaned out the lost and found. You claimed an orphan."

They decided to take a vote. It was unanimous. Nobody wanted me to return the sweater. I went into my boss's office. "They told me not to give it back," I said. "They're afraid it will raise suspicions if the sweater suddenly appears. But I'll hand it over if you say so."

"I told you I'd go along with what the other girls decided."

She had? I didn't remember that, but I didn't argue. It all seemed odd, an exercise of morals that lay just beyond my ken. I didn't want to implicate others—or myself—as larcenous. They had all worked at the club longer than I had, and many worked more hours a week and had a lot more contact with the members. Their reasoning baffled me, but it also served my purposes. I wanted that sweater, and was pleased to have a reason, however flimsy, for keeping it.

We worked night after night that year; Christmas bash after Christmas bash, some with seventy-five or a hundred guests, some with three hundred and four hundred guests. Then, on December 23rd, the night of the members' big Christmas party, we waitresses came in early to do our yearly gift exchange. From all those long, tough hours together, we knew each other well, and had gift-giving down to an art. I still remember how I got exactly the things I longed for from those women. This year, my boss handed me a soft package wrapped in tissue paper.

The contents of that package still sits next to the navy blue sweater at the bottom of my cedar chest. Inside the tissue I had found a long, hand-knit scarf in nubbly wool and mohair dyed in dark, saturated purples and magentas—and a familiar deep navy blue. "I was half finished knitting it when the owner came forward," said my boss. "When you were in there talking to the other waitresses about what to do about the sweater, I was sitting in my office and praying you wouldn't give it back."

That was more than twenty years ago. I wore that scarf as religiously as I wore the navy blue cashmere sweater—it hung right inside my closet on a hook; I can still recall the muscular movement of lifting it and twirling it around my neck. Unfortunately, it was particularly hard hit by the infestation of moths that ate huge holes in all the mohair items I'd had stored and folded in my closet. It's as holey as the sweater, and as useless, but the two sit there together at the bottom of the chest, beneath all subsequent cashmere and history, and remind me of a time of backbreaking work and the odd, fierce, hard-won friendship and camaraderie that came with it— when my friends knew better than I exactly what I wanted.

Michelle Huneven

Contributors

Bruce Bauman's ("It's Not the Knit, It's the Notion") work has appeared in numerous anthologies and magazines. His novel *And The Word Was* will be published by the Other Press/Handsel Press. He is an adjunct professor in the Cal Arts MFA Critical Studies program.

Joan Bond ("Grammy and Me") was born in Miami, Florida, on June 9, 1936. A native, she calls her hometown "Miama," not "Miamee" like the latecomers do. Married to her high-school sweetheart, Don, they celebrated their fiftieth last October. She has a daughter, Debbie, a son Timm, and two grandchildren, Valerie and Robert. She's had six careers beside being wife and mother: salesclerk, registered nurse, pilot, accountant, licensed real estate broker, and proprietor of a sewing store. Now she hopes she's left enough time in her life for a seventh career, that of writer.

Gayle Brandeis ("When you knit my sweater") is the author of *Fruitflesh: Seeds of Inspiration for Women Who Write* (HarperSanFrancisco) and *The Book of Dead Birds: A Novel* (HarperCollins). She lives in Riverside, California, with her husband and their two children.

Leah Buturain Schneider ("My Father's Scarf") is a gerontologist studying arts and theology at the Graduate Theological Union in Berkeley. She is a lecturer in the humanities and aging at the Leonard Davis School of Gerontology, USC in Los Angeles where her four children wish she would do more sitting and knitting.

Joanne Catz Hartman ("The Square Truth") writes and attempts to knit in Oakland, California, where she lives with her husband, daughter, and a dog of knitted collars. She is a columnist and editor for the online literary journal *Literary Mama*.

Ellen Chavez Kelley ("The Shawl"), poet and author of books and stories for young readers, has taught writing at UCSB, Santa Barbara's Adult Education program, and as a California Poet in the Schools. Her poems have appeared in many literary journals and anthologies. Her children's books include *The Lucky Lizard* (Dutton, 2000) and the forthcoming *Buckamoo Girls* (Harry N. Abrams, Inc.). Ellen lives in Santa Barbara, California, with her husband and her cat, Antoine.

Suzanne M. Cody ("Knit Think") knits and thinks in Iowa City, Iowa.

Karen Damskey and Leslie Stormon ("Fifteen-Yarn Sweater") are co-owners of L'Atelier, a successful retail and mail order company founded twenty-eight years ago. Both natives of Southern California, their designs are often said to have a California bend. Leslie's drawings and Karen's color sense and patterning come together in a unique partnership. Featured in *Vogue Knitting, Zen and the Art of Knitting*, and *Knitter's Stash*, they are well known in the knitting world.

Catherine Davis ("Dropped Stitches") is a knitter of forty-three years and lives in Enfield, New Hampshire. She reports that she's happily back on her way to knitting every day.

Cindy Dorn ("Kathleen's Scarf") was born and raised in Pasadena, California, where she still lives with her daughter Lily and their cat Whiskers. She works at the *Los Angeles Times* newspaper. Happily, she's recently learned to knit.

Melissa Garrison Elliott ("Six and Counting"), forty-eight, is a movie title designer and a writer of articles, essays, and stories. She has been published in *Voyages 2003*, *Veggie Life* magazine, *The Downtown News*, and *The Advocate*. She has lived in Los Angeles for 25 years.

Rebecca (Bekka) Gnewikow ("Why I Knit") is thirteen-and-a-half years old and will be in the eighth grade this school year. She lives in La Crosse, Wisconsin.

Karen J. Gordon ("A Stitch Held in Eternity") is a freelance writer and natural healing practitioner living in Eugene, Oregon. She writes articles and essays on the art and craft of writing and about her personal experiences with natural healing and other matters close to her heart. "A Stitch Held in Eternity" is excerpted from her book in progress, *Loving Theresa*. Her Web site is *www.karenjgordon.com*.

Libbie Greer ("K2, YO, P2") is a seventy-nine-year-old knitter, now living in Ashland, Oregon. Her daughter, Sylvia Greer, who's been knitting since age seven, helped her submit this story. Sylvia uses random knitting techniques to create felted wall sculptures and teaches "Free Range Knitting," an outdoor knitting class for intermediate and advanced knitters.

BJ Nathan Hegedus ("Tales of an Afghan") lives in Los Angeles and is currently working on a collection of essays about her childhood in N.Y.C.

Peggy Hong ("Inheritance") lives in Milwaukee, Wisconsin, with her three teens and her husband. She is the author of a poetry chapbook, *The Sister Who Swallows the Ocean* (CrowLadies, 1999) and *Three Truths and a Lie*, a collection of poems and stories. She teaches creative writing classes and workshops to people of all ages, children through adults.

Juleigh Howard-Hobson ("Tea Cosy") learned to knit as a girl in Australia, although she now lives and writes in the Pacific Northwest. She can be reached at *heyitsdarkinhere@yahoo.com*.

Michelle Huneven ("The Orphan Sweater") is the author of two novels, *Jamesland* (Knopf, 2003), and *Round Rock* (Knopf, 1997), which was named a *New York Times* Notable Book and a *Los Angeles Times* Best Book of the Year. She is presently a restaurant reviewer for the *LA Weekly*.

Tara Ison's ("Hands") novel, *A Child out of Alcatraz* (Faber & Faber, Inc., 1997), was a finalist for the *Los Angeles Times* Book Awards. She lives in Los Angeles, and she thinks she's been knitting since she was eight.

Jennifer Jameson ("The K1, P2 Profile") is a technical writer, dance enthusiast, and long-time knitter. She lives in Los Angeles with an embarrassing yarn stash and growing collection of Latin dance shoes. "The K1, P2 Profile" is her first published essay.

Liesl Jobson ("Knitting and the Farm Invasions") is a policewoman who plays flute in the SAPS Band in Soweto, South Africa. She is the script-writer for a new initiative using musical presentations at schools to assist the police in crime prevention, and to increase awareness of HIV/AIDS and sexual abuse of women and children. Her poetry and fiction have appeared in numerous online literary 'zines.

Rebecca Margaret Kuder ("Fit"), who holds an MFA in creative writing from Antioch University Los Angeles, has had stories published by *West Wind Review*. She lives in Yellow Springs, Ohio, where currently, between knitting projects, she is revising a novel.

Kathleen Lohr ("the secret of perfect tension") is a poet and professional screenwriter who lives in Los Angeles.

John P. McCann ("The Big Sweater") is a three-time Emmy Award–winning animation writer and producer. He lives in the hills above Los Angeles with his wife and a backyard full of deer (or "living venison") and he is working on a book of short stories about Hollywood.

Elisa Merkl ("Mother") was born in Portugal and lives in Goleta, California. She is an award-winning playwright, with nine produced plays to her credit (some coauthored), and her poetry has appeared in *Rivertalk* and *The Sower*.

Brenda Miller ("Knitted") is the author of a collection of essays, *Season of the Body* (Sarabande Books) that was a finalist for the PEN American Center Book Award. A three-time Pushcart Prize winner for her creative nonfiction work, Ms. Miller is an assistant professor of English at West Washington University and editor-in-chief of the *Bellingham Review*.

Mary Anne Mitchell ("Out of Chaos: A Knitter's Journey") is a knitter in British Columbia, Canada. Her writing has appeared in the online magazine *Knitty.com*.

Jennifer D. Munro ("A Knitter in Hawaii") was born and raised in Hawaii as a fourth-generation islander. She enjoys basket-weaving, juggling, and motorcycling. Excerpts from her memoir about miscarriage, *Not Suitable for Children*, have appeared in *Calyx*, *Kalliope*, *Room of One's Own*, *Slow Trains*, and *Clean Sheets*.

Amana Nova ("If These Yarns Could Speak") is a sweater designer in Southern California. Having lived in Asia for many years, she has grown to love the people and culture of that part of the world, as well as the beautiful things they make. She is now the owner of Mango Moon, which imports hand-spun, silk yarns from Nepal.

Leslie Petrovski ("Pass It On") is a freelance writer and beginning knitting teacher, who thinks about knitting when she writes and thinks about writing when she knits. She has written for *Vogue Knitting*, *Natural Home Magazine*, *The Christian Science Monitor*, and *The Denver Post* and is working on her first novel. She and her husband divide their time between Denver and Silver Cliff, Colorado.

Norah Piehl ("The Best-Laid Plans"), a freelance writer and editor, has been writing a whole lot longer than she's been knitting, and her work has appeared in numerous print and online publications. She lives in Massachusetts with her husband, son, and rapidly growing yarn stash.

Nancy Rabinowitz ("Crafty") is a freelance television writer living in New York City with her husband and three-year-old twins. Her work has appeared on Lifetime, HBO, A&E, and in the magazine *Brain, Child*. She's especially proud of having learned to knit in the dark. After all, with two kids and a job, she can pretty much only knit at night.

E. M. Ritt ("Mawk") lives in Kissimmee, Florida, where she has been involved in the arts for many years. She loves to write, sculpt, and paint.

Deborah Robson ("Traveling Socks") is a writing coach and book designer in Fort Collins, Colorado. She also designs knitwear; her original sock pattern is featured in Chapter 4.

Robyn Samuels ("The Endearing Elegance of Female Friendship") is a full-time mother, part-time writer, and storyteller living in Los Angeles with her husband and two daughters. She can knit squares.

Barbara Selesnick ("Preemie and Newborn Eyelet Cap") has been a flight attendant for Continental Airlines for twenty-six years. She's happily married, and also shares her home with a cat named Nike. She regularly attends knitting conventions and is an active knitter for charity, creating items for premature babies for Stitches from the Heart, as well as chemo hats for those suffering from cancer.

David Starkey ("Flame Stitch") is the author of the play *Soccer Moms*, and several collections of poetry, including *Fear of Everything*. He lives in Santa Barbara, California, with his wife, Sandy.

Leslie Stormon ("Fifteen-Yarn Sweater Pattern")—see listing with Karen Damskey.

Linda Urban ("Bootie Call") is marketing director for Vroman's Bookstore, one of the nation's oldest and largest independents. She, her husband, Julio, and her daughter, Claire, live in Pasadena, California, in a Craftsman bungalow with too few bookshelves and not nearly enough closet space for her yarn stash.

Irene Wanner ("The Red Guernsey") teaches fiction writing in Seattle at Richard Hugo House and the UW Women's Center. She reviews books for *The Seattle Times* and *The San Francisco Chronicle*, serves as an editor for *The Seattle Review*, and is a member of the Northwest Independent Editors Guild.

Helen Wright Davis ("Quiet Please—Knitting Zone") began to both knit and write poetry at age four. This is the first narrative effort for the Canadian mother of three and grandmother of seven. She was helped in this endeavor by Judi Davis Healey, whose last knitting effort was for a long-gone high-school flame. Judi is a UCLA Writing Project Fellow and a Los Angeles County Teacher of the Year. Judi's dad and Helen, both widowed after more than fifty years of marriage, are now celebrating their second wedding anniversary.